ISO 9000:2000

An Implementation Guide
(Includes a Self-Assessment Checklist)

Praveen Gupta, PE, ASQ Fellow

This book is available at a quantity discount when purchased in bulk. For more information, contact:

Accelper Consulting
1320, Tower Road, Suite 139
Schaumburg, IL 60173

(847) 884-1900
Fax: (847) 884-7280
E-mail: info@accelper.com

Second Edition

Publisher	- Book Surge
Editor	- Arvin Sri
Cover Artist	- Dan Pongetti

Printed in the United States of America

ISBN 1-4196-2743-0

About the Author

Praveen Gupta, President of Accelper Consulting, has been working in the quality field since 1980. He worked at Motorola in the Semiconductor Product Sector and Communications Sector and at AT&T Bell Laboratories for nine years. He founded Accelper Consulting (formerly Quality Technology Company) in 1989 to provide training and consulting services to businesses. Accelper Consulting has been focusing on the process approach in implementing ISO 9001 for many years before it was formalized in its 2000 version. He participated in the development of the ISO 9000: 2000 version of the standard.

Praveen developed the Process Control Standard for IPC and provides training and consulting in ISO 9001/TS-16949/ISO 14001. He has trained executives for Motorola University in Six Sigma, Design for Manufacturability, Cycle Time Reduction (Lean), Statistical Process Control and Managing Continuous Improvement. Praveen and his team of consultants have developed expertise in quickly and easily implementing effective quality management systems.

Praveen holds an MSEE in Computer Engineering from the Illinois Institute of Technology, Chicago, and is a CQE, a CSQE and a PE in Illinois. He is also an ASQ Fellow. Praveen has published several books including his best selling – Six Sigma Business Scorecard, has published articles on Quality, Six Sigma and Innovation in many magazines, and has presented at conferences nationwide.

Praveen can be contacted at Accelper Consulting at (847) 884-1900 or by email at praveen@accelper.com.

Foreword

The ISO 9000 based quality systems have been implemented for more than ten years. Its adoption by businesses worldwide has been growing rapidly. As companies implemented the ISO 9000 quality management system, they observed a need for changes to make the standard more value-added and easy to implement. The ISO 9001:2000 system provides such a standard.

The ISO 9000:2000 An Implementation Guide provides an excellent road map for installing a value-added quality management system and how to conduct good internal audits. Mr. Gupta explains the current business situations in the Introduction. The ISO 9001:2000 Getting Ready section presents hints to implement the new system cost effectively. Beyond quality and Cost/Benefits are discussed in the last two chapters. Finally, an excellent Checklist to help companies assess their readiness for compliance to the ISO 9001:2000 standard, or migrate their registration to the new standard, is included.

This book provides excellent and practical information to implement quality and environmental management systems effectively. I enjoyed reading the book and believe it offers significant value to anyone who is interested in improving the management system of his/her organization.

Frank Brletich,
Associate Dean
Lake Forest Graduate School of Management

Acknowledgements

I would like to acknowledge my colleagues – Arvin Sri, Karen Fletcher, Jit Lodd and Dan Pongetti, as well as organizations such as IPC, Spring Manufacturers Institute, PCFAB (CMP Media), and ASQ Press for publishing the following articles, the contents of which have been utilized in writing this book.

Implementing a Value-Added Quality System – Praveen Gupta and Jit Lodd, Spring Industry Technical Symposium, 1999

Conducting Value-Added Internal Audits – Karen Fletcher and Praveen Gupta, Printed Circuit Fabrication, November 1999

Are ISO/QS-9000 Certifications Worth the Time and Money? – Praveen Gupta and Dan Pongetti, Quality Progress, October, 1998

Ready for Version Y2K of ISO 9000? – Praveen Gupta, PCFAB, April 2000

Cost Effective Implementation of ISO 14001 – Praveen Gupta, presented at IPC PCB Expo, 1999.

Special thanks to Al Alonzo, Celeste Nair, Terry Luczak, and Terri Furgiuele for critically reviewing the book.

I would especially like to thank my wife Archana, and my children Avanti and Krishna, who have been inspiring me to do better in my personal quality improvement process.

Being in a quality profession is a demanding job that requires a strong positive attitude in order to succeed. I therefore present this book to quality professionals who work without authority, who work hard, and who are dedicated to making their organizations the best in class.

Praveen Gupta

Preface

Quality is an integral part of life and business. Without quality of work, quality of life and quality of people, the society cannot function effectively. Quality standards have become a norm in today's business. The release of the new ISO 9001:2000 standard requires us to re-learn the intent of the original ISO 9000 standards.

With a release of any standard or its revision, awareness to the standard must be raised, and requirements must be understood. It requires practical experience to elaborate the ISO 9001:2000 standard's requirements. Praveen Gupta, who has more than 25 years of experience practicing various aspects of quality management systems, shares his lessons with the reader.

The book, ISO 9000: 2000 An Implementation Guide, has been structured so that it enables the reader to understand the ISO 9001:2000 standard, as well as how to implement an effective quality management system. The book explains key management processes including management review, internal audit and corrective action.

The checklist and associated method to assess a company's quality management system is an excellent treatment of the standard. The checklist is easy to understand and includes an explanation for each question. The author also discusses ISO 14001 standards that are in alignment with the new ISO 9000 standards.

Finally, the reader makes the book more valuable by applying some of the principles at work. The book is only as good as its reader's desire is to use it. I am sure you will find this book useful in implementing your quality management system and beyond.

Table of Contents

Thinking of Quality...

Business is a collection of processes.

Process is a set of activities.

Quality is a measure of performance of activities.

Quality is a thought to do the job well in each activity.

Quality management is getting the job done well.

Quality is the business of top management.

Quality is everyone's business.

Quality is not in the eye of the beholder anymore.
Quality is in the hearts of customers.
Quality is in the heads of employees.
Quality is in the hands of management.

- Praveen Gupta

Introduction

Since the release of the ISO 9000 standards in 1987, over five hundred thousands of companies have achieved registration in just over 13 years. The ISO 9000 standards series was easily accepted due to its flexibility in implementation, simplicity of requirements, and of course, market demand or competitive reasons.

Results have been mixed so far. In working with several companies, I have found that many companies have been certified to ISO 9000; however, they have no interest in the standard or in their quality management system. In other words, their commitment to quality is an unrealistic expectation.

The 1987 version of the standard, comprising the twenty famous elements, included documenting the system, implementing the system, conducting internal audits and taking corrective actions. We have all heard the anonymous quote, "Document what you do, and do what you document." This saying really did a lot of harm to the ISO 9000 standards and misled consultants, management, and registrars alike. The underlying premise that you do well before documenting is not always assumed. However, if we take the time to understand what needs to be done right, and then we document what we do, the above quote is a good one.

Many registrars focus on compliance rather than effectiveness. As a result, companies are certified without any added value, with less meaningful documentation, and with no change in the processing of the product. There is no change in the way work is done at the company. Therefore the company's ability to realize quality objectives is questionable.

The new version of the ISO 9000 standards consists of the following documents:

ANSI/ASQ Q9000-2000: Quality management systems – Fundamentals and vocabulary
ANSI/ASQ Q9004-2000: Quality management systems – Guidelines for performance improvement
ANSI/ASQ Q9001-2000: Quality management systems – Requirements

The above standards are listed in the order of significance to aid in better understanding the quality management system. The new ISO 9001:2000 version has considered input from various sources about the effectiveness of the standard in general. Focus has shifted from documentation to a process-based model for effectiveness. The emphasis has changed from focusing on procedures to focusing on methods to collect, analyze and act on data. The requirements have been reorganized and regrouped based on the process model.

According to the process model, any activity, or set of activities, that uses resources to transform inputs to outputs can be considered a process. For a company to effectively implement a quality management system, it needs to identify and manage various processes and their interactions. The output of one process is an input to another process. In order to implement a company-wide quality management system, the company must implement process management at each process (function or subsystem) level.

To manage a process, the process owner needs to control inputs, in-process and output as shown in Figure 1 below. The control means understanding requirements, and receiving, producing or supplying according to the requirements. To ensure compliance to the requirements at various stages, verification methods are implemented. The verification methods could be controlling suppliers and/or monitoring product or process through data analysis, inspection, test or measurements. If the verification shows that the requirements are not met, a corrective action needs to be initiated.

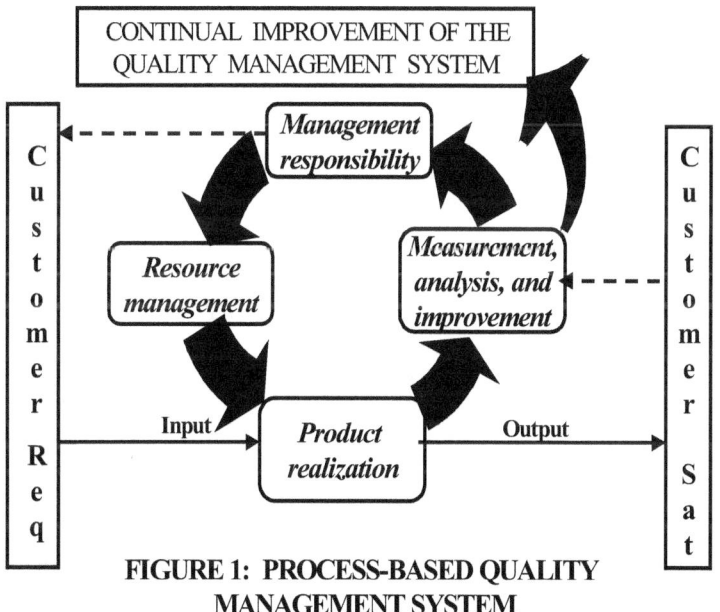

**FIGURE 1: PROCESS-BASED QUALITY
MANAGEMENT SYSTEM**

Once we learn to manage a process effectively, we must identify critical process steps throughout operations, verify them, ensure their compliance to the requirements, and produce acceptable results.

After defining responsibility and ownership of the processes definition and documentation, employee training, good data collection, data analysis and corrective actions one can manage the process effectively, according to the intent of the new version of ISO 9001:2000.

If roles and responsibility for each and every employee are defined and documented, and accountability is established, the company management can smoothly run the business with the process management mentality. Of course, if not watched, the quality management system can be blamed for all the problems. With process management, the difference between employees and management disappears. Everyone, including management, must perform their assigned task(s) according to the intent and processes of quality management system. With this synergy and harmony, the company develops an effective quality management system that can facilitate growth, down sizing and re-growth equally well. A well-run quality management system should make the company perform like a 'well-oiled' machine.

Besides process management, another change that is apparent in the new version of the standard is the focus on data collection and analysis for making decisions. This change has been expressed in terms of identifying various processes and their interrelations, monitoring and measuring at critical processes, and reviewing data and results for effectiveness throughout (as well as in the management review meeting) to identify opportunities for improvement. In order to implement the new version, one must clearly define data collection methods, filing methods and periodic analysis throughout the organization.

Shifting the focus from compliance to effectiveness will have tremendous impact during implementation and during audits (both internal and registration). Some companies will take the path of least resistance to comply with the requirements instead of their intent. Registrars must ensure their auditors are trained, have experience looking into the intent of the system, and demand proper implementation of the quality management system. If not, compliance becomes even harder to achieve, the perception of the standards is relaxed, and eventually the purpose of the standard revision is lost. Auditing against the intent of the standard is going to be a challenge for organizations to implement and registrars to verify for registration. The Registrar Accreditation Board (RAB) must ensure that variation among registrars is minimized for the best value to society.

Finally, the success or failure of any initiative in an organization depends upon the leadership. The responsibility of 'top' management has been more clearly defined and documented in ISO 9001:2000. The 'top' management must take the attitude that this quality system is its business to run. It is a wonderful tool to really manage the business without losing sight of the company's profitability. Instead of saying, "What does quality have to do with business?" top management must believe and demonstrate that quality, or doing a job well, is everything a business must offer to customers. Customers will take care of your profitability if less waste exists in the supply chain.

Implementing an Effective Quality System

History of ISO 9000

In 1987, the first edition of the ISO 9000 standard was released by the International Organization for Standardization (ISO). Since its foundation, ISO has developed over 10,000 standards, among which the ISO 9000 standard is the most widely accepted in the world today. The ISO 9000 series of standards was developed to help companies throughout the world adopt a common ground for implementing a value-added quality system.

Since the 'birth' of quality concepts in the business world, a variety of quality system standards have been developed and used by companies throughout the world to meet and/or exceed customer expectations. The increased number of standards to achieve a common goal of consistency in quality of services or products produced raised a few simple questions: Why not have one standard that all of us can follow? Is it so difficult to develop one? These questions were answered when the ISO 9000 standard was released.

The ISO 9000 standard is based on a collection of sound commonsensical business practices. The standard addresses all aspects of the business functions, including, but not limited to, sales, design, purchasing, manufacturing, servicing and management, with the exception of finance. Today there have been more than 300,000 ISO 9000 certifications issued in the world. Over 50,000 certifications are held by companies in the United States.

Value vs. Paper Monster

When people hear about ISO 9000, some think of it as a tool to improve processes, others think of it as a paper monster, and still others think of it as beneficial but bureaucratic. A survey conducted by Quality Technology Company found that the most commonly stated benefit appears to be the improvement of the quality system. The top five benefits of the ISO/QS-9000 based quality system as identified in the survey[1] are as follows:

> Improves quality system
> Provides consistency
> Broadens customer base
> Builds customer confidence
> Improves organizational structure

Initially, when the standards were released in 1987, the intent was to implement a quality system based on the ISO 9004-1, titled Guidelines to implement quality system, which also included cost of quality. Then based on the market requirements, a certification model could be selected. The main purpose of implementing a quality system has been to:

> Establish a quality focus that is geared to achieve business objectives.
> Develop policies and procedures that support business operations.

Instead, in reality, companies joined the bandwagon and rushed for registration by documenting practices for compliance. Registrar's auditors then verified the practices, and the company got certified. However, the effectiveness or the usefulness of the documented practices in meeting business objectives remained unaffected. As a result, perceptions have been established about ISO 9000 registration such as:

➢ What has ISO 9000 got to do with business?
➢ I just want to get certified. I do not have time to do it the right way.
➢ Our quality did not get better; actually, we get more customer complaints. We are ISO 9002 certified.
➢ I know some of our suppliers who are ISO 9000 certified. They ship worse products now than they used to. They believe the problems are due to paperwork or lack of time for ISO 9000.
➢ It's a lot of paperwork. It is slowing us down in doing our work. We need to simplify the ISO 9000 system. (Sounds familiar for a cost reduction program; remember that costs are more than the savings.)
➢ An ISO 9000 system is for manufacturers only, not for service companies.
➢ An ISO 9000 system is expensive to implement. Our customers do not want to pay for it.
➢ Our customers don't care; all they want is for us to be certified.

An analysis of the above comments to find the symptoms of failures brings the following to mind:

1. Management's Misunderstanding - The corporate management still does not understand that the ISO 9000 quality system in reality is a business management system. If drivers for implementing a quality system are correctly identified, the results could be different. Then the benefits would be visualized and realized using an ISO 9000 compliant quality system. The executive's interest and commitment is critical to make the ISO 9000 system a value-driven tool to reduce waste and improve quality.

The Management Responsibility requirement of ISO 9000 is utilized for compliance purpose, and is not utilized as intended. Ideally, the internal audits of the quality system must find opportunities for improvement, and the corrective action system must facilitate the improvement and remedy the nonconformances. The purpose of management review is to ensure that the internal audits and corrective actions are effectively implemented.

If the above three elements, namely management responsibility, internal audits and corrective actions, are properly implemented, the quality system is bound to improve and produce the desired results. Conversely, if these three elements are improperly implemented, damage is significant to the company's performance and also to the country's economy.

2. Consultant's Counseling - Consultants can prove to be an asset or a liability to the client in implementing an effective quality system. Given that consultants have a variety of backgrounds, the most important one is that the consultant must have proven experience in the quality field. The consultant must think from the company's, and not from the registrar's, perspective. Consultants who assist in developing and implementing a system that can be registered miss the intent and purpose of the quality system.

If, on the other hand, a consultant guides the development of a quality system considering business needs, the quality

9

system is bound to be value-added, and registration is guaranteed sooner or later. The benefits do not wait for registration, as the company starts realizing benefits even before registration. Therefore, anyone counseling to get certified as a main focus must be redirected to focus on effectiveness.

It has also been noticed through advertisements that a quality system registration can be obtained between three to six months. In real life, a quality system evolves over time – it is not bought or obtained overnight. The main principle of implementing an ISO 9000 system is to create quality thinking, i.e., raise awareness to do things right, rather than just doing them as usual. Had it been just for compliance, we might not have needed ISO 9000 in the first place.

Therefore, one must understand that the effective quality system, with or without the help of a consultant, must inspire more employee involvement and raise less resistance. The documentation and records must be integrated with the job, rather than created as a separate job altogether. Such a quality system will be less painful and more fruitful.

3. Registrar's Regression - The price of free market is that anyone with some money can become a registrar. It has been known that some companies just want to get certified. In other words, there are some registrars that will just meet that need of getting certified. It is the weakest link in the registration of the quality system.

Companies expect more thorough audits than the ones performed by some registrars. Due to fierce competition, the pressure is to please the customer by easing up on the audit.

However, it is not really easing up the audit; it is relapsing the audit just for the sake of compliance and not for effectiveness. Comments like "The audit was easy" or "They found nothing" are not uncommon. One can group the auditors into three categories as follows:

a. Literal Auditors - Here the auditors basically bring a checklist and quickly create records for their file to show to their management that they conducted the audit. In other words, they are more interested in their compliance than the compliance of the company they are auditing. These auditors are verifying compliance in a literal sense. In other words, they are looking for specific words in the documents in order to feel comfortable that they verified the quality system against the requirements. These auditors do not have experience in auditing quality systems.

b. Blind-Sided Auditors - Here the auditors go in a little late, look around, talk to a few people, complete their records and determine that a company is in compliance to the requirements. They take it easy, and let the client take it easy, in order to build a long-term business relationship. Again, here the intent is to complete the audit formalities rather than formally audit the system.

c. Intent-Oriented Auditors - In this category, the auditors understand the intent of the standards and implementation of the company's quality system. They audit the quality system for both compliance and effectiveness. In evaluating effectiveness, the auditors find opportunities for improvement and logical and meaningful disconnects, thus adding value to their customers. This is a bit painful in the short term, but in the long term, customers and auditees appreciate the audit findings.

4. Flaws in Implementation

a. Documentation - The main purpose of documentation is to maintain consistency and control the operations. Consistency relates to compliance and control relates to effectiveness. There is a saying in the ISO 9000 world, "Document what you do, and do what you document." Typically, the saying is interpreted in terms of consistency and not in terms of control or effectiveness. Therefore, the focus is to document whatever is being done to the most detailed level. This takes a long time, and the documents are of limited use. Instead, when documenting a quality system, the goal must be to document a company's quality system meaningfully so that the document serves its 'purpose.' Details in documentation must be based on the competency (training and skills) of the user of the document, not on that of the software used or the author. Otherwise, the company ends up having too much documentation of little value. The documentation then really looks like a paper monster, as it is too much to read and difficult to understand. Without a good understanding of documents, employees are reluctant to use the documents.

b. Ineffective Audits - At times, internal audits are performed just for compliance against poorly established procedures. The audit findings are trivial and create tons of paperwork. The audit frequency is inappropriate, the audit training is insufficient and the auditors are not qualified. All this leads to ineffective internal quality audits, in which case the audits do not add any value to the improvement of the quality system.

c. Incorrect Corrective Actions - Another major problem is that people do not take time to identify the root cause of the problem. Instead, they treat symptoms. Even worse, they start the corrective action request (CAR) form and file it for further processing. If followed correctly it would be beneficial. However, due to lack of understanding of the process, people write corrective actions that have nothing to do with the cause of the problem. As a result, the problem does not get fixed and paperwork is created, thus achieving virtual compliance. Generally, this causes a lot of frustration in the company, because it gives feelings of having a system that provides no real benefits or value.

d. Mismanaged Management Reviews - There is one thing the company's executive management must do personally for its profitability and for the quality system -- that is to take ownership of the management review process and not participate in a meeting for compliance purposes. Instead, use the management review meeting as a tool to see if the quality system is meeting the business and ISO 9000 requirements.

Implementation Approach

Following is how to implement an effective system:

1. Analyze Business Operations - The key to implementing a valued-added quality system is to understand how the current business operates, how the various processes within the business are linked and implemented, and how much of it is formally implemented. Understand the intent and requirements of the ISO 9000 standard, and identify the 'gap' between the standard and the business processes. Keep in mind that if a company has been in business for a certain number of years, it must be having some formal and good practices implemented.

2. Develop a Plan - Having recognized the company's strengths and identified opportunities for improvement, the next step is to develop a plan to bridge the 'gap' between the business operations and the requirements of the standard. Develop an implementation plan that clearly identifies the areas to be addressed by each element of the standard for documentation and implementation, the team/individuals responsible for those areas, and the target dates for completion. As the system evolves, the plan will change. Therefore, periodically review progress against the plan and update it.

3. Document Quality System - A typical question asked by many is: "What do we document?" The standard only tells 'what' to do and not 'how' to do it. Document the business processes to comply with the intent of the requirements and meet the business needs. It is critical that one documents the business processes without compromising the intent of the standard while, at the same time, not creating a paper monster. The objective of documenting the system is to ensure consistency in implementing business practices and minimize variation. Some practices must be changed, added or deleted from the existing ones in order to meet the intent of the standard. Another question asked by many is: "How much do we document?" Follow the KISS principle - keep it short and simple. The ISO 9001 standard gives a lot of flexibility in the amount of detail to be included in the documentation. We have heard some say, "The more you document, the more you open yourselves during the audit." Do not forget the objective of documentation - consistency and controls. Thus, it is very critical that the steps to be followed and the controls to ensure consistency and effectiveness are clearly defined. Obtain everybody's 'buy in' for the documentation by giving all those concerned ownership of processes. If outside consultants are assisting to document your system, make sure they work with the department personnel involved with the processes to realize the maximum benefit.

Generally, a good procedure must be able to address the following aspects of a process as shown in Figure 2 - Process model:

To implement a process, inputs (methods, machines, material and people) and certain process steps need to be followed, with established process controls, to generate an output. The output is then verified to ensure that it meets the input and process requirements. When the output meets the specified requirements, it is moved to the next stage of processing.

When the output does not meet the specified requirements, it is isolated, and some actions are taken to adjust the process steps or inputs. This approach can be followed to document any business process.

4. Train Employees - Implementing an ISO 9000-based quality system is definitely going to affect the culture positively within the organization. Therefore, prepare the employees through training and education to believe that the

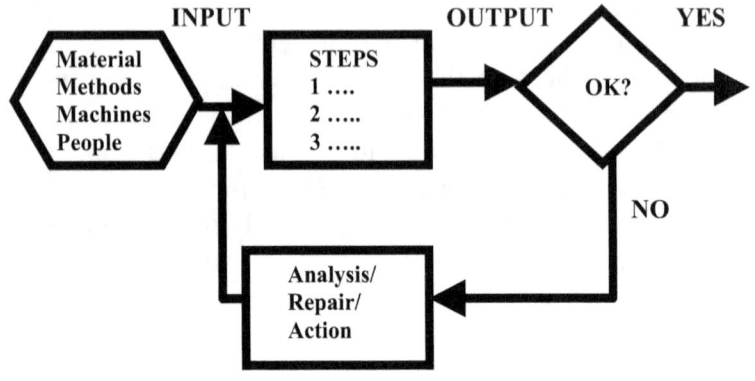

FIGURE 2: PROCESS MODEL

quality system is going to be implemented. Several types of training can be conducted at various levels of the organization, depending on the nature and complexity of the work force. Provide detailed training on understanding the intent and requirements of the standards to those who are going to be directly involved in the documentation process. Management and executives can spend about half a day to understand what is involved, the benefits and what it takes to get certified. Management must also understand the roles they must play in the system to make it worth the investment. Provide awareness training to production employees with an emphasis on the requirements pertaining to their functional area. With today's diverse cultural and ethnic workforces, provide training preferably in everyone's native language. Train a select group of qualified, experienced and analytical individuals to be internal auditors.

5. Implement System - Implementing the system poses numerous challenges to companies. Typical ones include: procedures not meeting the actual practice, lack of employee/management buy-in, lack of commitment, etc. To effectively implement the system, distribute the implementation responsibility to the department managers/supervisors. Give them the ownership, and make them responsible for implementing their share of the quality system. Avoid selecting one person for implementing the whole system – that will not work unless everyone is committed to it. Train the employees on the operating procedures and/or work instructions. Training can be in the classroom or at the work area itself. The latter approach is usually preferable, as employees generally feel more comfortable in their own 'space.'

6. Conduct Internal Audits – Develop an internal audit schedule/plan, keeping in mind the business objectives and importance of the quality system activities. Perform internal audits on time and as per the schedule. Keep in mind that the intent of internal auditing is to evaluate compliance and effectiveness as well as to take the necessary actions to correct the issue at hand, be it the practice or the documentation.

7. Take Corrective Actions - Use the corrective action system to address nonconformities in the process/system. This is the most powerful element of the standard that will provide real benefits when utilized correctly even before registration. A good corrective action process should address the following areas at a minimum: define problem, perform root cause analysis, take actions, verify effectiveness and close the corrective action request.

Perform a thorough investigation to understand what really happened and why. Refrain from asking the question: "Who did it?" This will blindfold one's vision to look deeper. Also, avoid the typical root causes such as "operator error," "misplaced," "employee forgot to implement," etc. How can one possibly correct these causes? Also, once the actions have been taken, verify the effectiveness of the actions to ensure that they were worth the time and money invested into them. If there is sufficient evidence to support the effectiveness, only then close the action. Closing corrective actions without verifying effectiveness is a common pitfall of many quality systems.

8. Conduct Management Review - This is so vital that without effective management review, the quality system is going to degrade over time. An effective management review means the right frequency, right agenda, right action items, right attendees, and right intent. Absence of any one 'right' will lead to fruitless management reviews. The right frequency is not once a year. The right agenda must include effectiveness of internal audits and corrective actions, the right action items must include clear responsibility and target completion date(s), the right attendees must include the company's president (not always his/her designee), and the right intent means personal commitment to make the quality system work. If done correctly, the management review can directly lead to improvement in the quality system and thus the company's performance.

Management Anatomy - Internal audits act as management's eyes and ears, corrective and preventive actions act as management's arms and legs, and the management review is management's head and heart for providing direction. (See

Figure 3.) The internal audits find nonconformances or opportunities for improvement, corrective and preventive actions remedy the faults in the quality system or improve the process, and the management review ensures that internal audits and corrective actions are working effectively and in harmony.

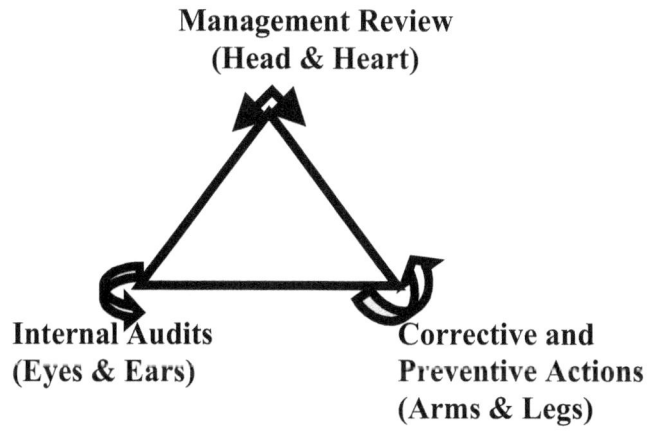

Management Review
(Head & Heart)

Internal Audits
(Eyes & Ears)

Corrective and
Preventive Actions
(Arms & Legs)

FIGURE 3: MANAGEMENT ANATOMY

In order to implement a useful quality system, several factors have to be considered. Documentation is a major effort, but every element and all aspects must be documented correctly. One needs to select a right registrar, have internal auditing training that focuses on compliance and effectiveness, have the 'right' management review process, an effective training program, and good record keeping. Most important of all, everyone in the company must understand the right intent of the quality system.

Since quality is everyone's job, every process is included in the quality system. If one visualizes it, the quality system is a powerful business management tool. Therefore, the company management must take responsibility to ensure that the quality system is well defined, documented and implemented. Otherwise, it is a disservice to the company and the society.

Future of ISO 9000

The ISO 9000 standards have been revised with the business needs in mind. This new focus has several similarities in terms of structure and organization to the Malcolm Baldrige National Quality Award (MBNQA) criteria. The revised standards are easier to understand and use, especially for the traditionally non-manufacturing type of industries. The ISO 9001:2000 standard has reorganized the 20 elements of the ISO 9001 standard into 5 main clauses. A few new requirements, specifically customer satisfaction assessment and continual improvement, have been added. The ISO 9001:2000 has also been aligned with the ISO 14001 standards for environmental management systems. The language and terminology have also been changed to make the standard easier to understand and more acceptable to the businesses worldwide.

What is the future of ISO 9000? This is a current question in an industry with different beliefs and perceptions. Some believe that the ISO 9000 wave - as they call it - will last forever, while others think that it is just another 'wave' and will soon recede. The QTC survey (as published in Quality Progress) shows that only 35% of certified companies and 36% of non-certified companies believe that another standard will replace it. This survey also shows that 57% of companies plan to get certified within the next five years.

The benefits of implementing an ISO 9000 based quality system far outweigh the disadvantages that any other standards have shown in the world today. It is no doubt that the ISO 9000 standards have established a strong foothold in the industry and are here to stay for years and even decades to come. Of course, this will only happen if companies implement the standard for its true intent, which is to establish a value-added quality system, and not merely for the certificate.

Reference

1. Praveen Gupta and Dan Pongetti, "Are ISO/QS-9000 Certifications Worth the Time and Money?" Quality Progress, October 1998.

ISO 9001:2000,
TS-16949 and QS-9000

The advent of ISO 9000 quality management standards really started the age of standardization. Prior to ISO 9000, confusion existed because of annual quality programs. Many companies had started SPC, JIT, TQM, and Zero Defect type programs that produced limited results and consumed huge resources.

In the early eighties (i.e., the prime time for quality programs) nobody knew what worked consistently. Thanks to the unification of Europe (that necessitated the unified quality standards), the age of standardization started. The International Organization of Standardization (ISO) has been developing standards for the last 50 years. ISO 9000 started the age of standardization and involved everybody in companies.

After the release of the ISO 9000 series, a new industry of consultants, trainers and other organizations was born. Quality leaders in large corporations (including those in the automotive industry) believed that their needs had not been considered in the development of ISO 9000 standards. Therefore, they resisted the change to comply with the ISO 9000 standards.

QS-9000 is a standard that was developed based on the ISO 9000 standard. The difference between them is that while the ISO 9000 standard is eight pages long, the QS-9000 document is about 100 pages long and supported by 5 reference manuals. The reasons for ISO 9000's prompt acceptance include its simplicity and non-prescriptive nature. Businesses had flexibility in implementing requirements of ISO 9000 as they deemed fit.

QS-9000, on the other hand, has more requirements. The QS-9000 standard calls for certain requirements to be implemented in a certain way. Having worked with many companies as a consultant, those requirements have been very difficult to implement due to required resources. Since customers demand QS-9000 (who do not practice it themselves), the suppliers get registered. However, a lot needs to be done to accomplish the intent of QS-9000.

The challenges are how to maintain QS-9000 in harmony with the ISO 9000 standard. The revised ISO 9001:2000 version has been released; now the QS-9000 standard needs to be revised, or left unchanged, or de-linked from ISO 9000. If harmonized with ISO 9000, the intent of standardization is maintained. If de-linked from the ISO 9001:2000 standard, de-standardization begins, and that will mark the end of the standardization age. Some new programs need to be identified such as Six Sigma, but this is not the author's recommendation!

With the recognition of the QS-9000 standard due to resources pumped into it, other industries started their own variations of the ISO 9000 standard. Some of them are AS-9000 (Aerospace), TL-9000 (Telecommunication), and MD-9000 (Medical Devices). Fundamentally, the business' main requirements are the same. For some unique implementation of an industry requirement, which could easily be included in the scope of ISO 9001:2000, creating a new standard with limited added value will prove to be counterproductive. It will consume the industry's resources, it will sicken owners to their stomach, and it will create a lot of waste in the name of quality. The end seems visible: the decline of the ISO 9000 standard.

With the release of ISO 9001:2000, the main difference between QS-9000 and ISO 9000 remains in the area of significance of records and facts-based decision-making. QS-9000's Competitive Analysis and Benchmarking Requirements have given enough evidence that such requirements are hard to implement, difficult to audit, and add little to no value. These requirements are not the natural acts to follow in a business without an effective fundamental structure.

ISO 9001:2000 incorporates some aspects of QS-9000, such as customer satisfaction, data analysis and quality planning. In this regard, the QS-9000 standard has contributed towards the improvement of the ISO 9000 standard.

Organizations have a challenge. If they are QS-9000 certified, and they want to maintain ISO 9000 registration, they need to revise the ISO 9000-based requirements of their quality system to maintain certification to ISO 9001:2000.

Otherwise, companies will get certified to ISO 9000, but some will be certified to the old version and some to the new version. That is really what ISO 9000-type quality standards intend to prevent - a global document control problem.

Analysis of ISO 9001:2000 and QS-9000 standards:

ISO 9001:2000 requirements	Related QS-9000 requirements
Quality management system	
General requirements	4.2
Documentation requirements	4.2, 4.5, 4.16
Management responsibility	
Management commitment	4.1
Customer focus	4.1
Quality policy	4.1
Planning	4.1, 4.2
Responsibility, authority and communication	4.1
Management review	4.1
Resource management	
Provision of resources	4.1
Human Resources	4.1
Infrastructure	4.2, 4.9
Work environment	4.9
Product realization	
Planning of product realization	4.1, 4.2
Customer-related processes	4.1, 4.2, 4.3, Section II, 4.14
Design and development	4.4
Purchasing	4.6
Production and service provision	4.2, 4.7, 4.8, 4.9, 4.15, 4.19
Control of monitoring and measuring devices	4.11

ISO 9001:2000 requirements	Related QS-9000 requirements
Measurement, analysis and improvement	
General	4.1, 4.16, 4.20
Monitoring and measurement	4.1, 4.17, 4.9, 4.10
Control of nonconforming product	4.13
Analysis of data	4.1, 4.16
Improvement	4.2, 4.14

ISO/TS-16949

The goal of this technical specification is to align QS-9000 requirements with those of the global automotive industry. ISO/TS-16949 is based on the ISO 9001:2000 version. This technical specification can be also applied throughout the automotive supply chain. TS-16949 builds on the ISO 9001:2000 and QS-9000 standards. The unique requirements specifically identified in ISO/TS-16949 are the following:

➢ Customer representative
➢ Employee motivation, empowerment and satisfaction
➢ Impact on society including product safety and regulations
➢ Management of process design
➢ Process improvement
➢ Quality system improvement
➢ Design optimization
➢ Returned product test/analysis
➢ Training on the job

The ISO 9001:2000 standard does align itself with the QS-9000, ISO/TS-16949 and ISO 14001 requirements. However, from an organization's perspective that is serving customers in multiple industries and multiple countries, just hearing the number of quality management standards is a discouraging fact. They certainly wish that only one quality management system standard existed -- that is ISO 9001:2000.

ISO 9001:2000 – Getting Ready

ISO 9000 standards have been in existence since 1987. The number of companies implementing the quality system and achieving registration has been growing since its release. Several hundreds of thousands of organizations have achieved ISO 9000 registration and are benefiting from it. Now the standards have been changed to achieve even better quality.

Surveys have found that the most commonly stated benefits of implementing ISO 9000 quality systems include the following:

➢ Improved product quality
➢ Consistency, standardization and repeatability
➢ Increased business
➢ Builds customer confidence
➢ Better management and less confusion in the plant

Besides gaining all the benefits of implementing an effective quality system, there are opportunities for improvement with the current requirements of the standards. Some of the industry-wide concerns include the following:

➢ Lots of documentation or paperwork
➢ There is no change in doing the business
➢ Management does not care
➢ Quality has not improved

The standards committee heard all the issues and revised the standard. They devised a new standard that has been reviewed by many companies, consultants and registrars.

The result of the committee's efforts: the ISO 9001:2000 version was released in December 2000.

The new standards re-emphasize the process approach and facts-based decision-making. The process approach consists of four major elements: Management Responsibility, Resource Management, Product Realization, and Measurement, Analysis and Improvement. The model recognizes the significant role played by customers in defining requirements as inputs and providing feedback to validate that the requirements have been met.

The previously published three models of the ISO 9000 standards have been merged into the new ISO 9001:2000 standard. Also, the current terminology of subcontractor, supplier and customer has been replaced by supplier, organization and customer, respectively.

The most obvious change in the new standard is that there are no longer twenty requirements. The requirements have been regrouped as follows:

Quality management system
➢ General requirements
➢ Documentation requirements – General, Quality manual, Control of documents, Control of records

Management responsibility
➢ Management commitment
➢ Customer focus
➢ Quality policy
➢ Planning – Quality objectives, Quality management system planning

- ➤ Responsibility, authority and communication – Responsibility and authority, Management representative, Internal communication
- ➤ Management review – General, Review input, Review output

Resource management
- ➤ General
- ➤ Provision of resources
- ➤ Human resources – General, Competence, Awareness and training, Infrastructure, Work environment

Product realization
- ➤ Planning of product realization
- ➤ Customer-related processes – Determination of requirements related to the product, Review of requirements related to the product, Customer communication
- ➤ Design and development – Planning, Inputs, Outputs, Review, Verification, Validation, Control of changes
- ➤ Purchasing – Purchasing process, Purchasing information, Verification of purchased product
- ➤ Production and service provision – Control of production and service provision, Validation of processes for production and service operations, Identification and traceability, Customer property, Preservation of product
- ➤ Control of monitoring and measuring devices

Measurement, analysis and improvement
- ➤ General
- ➤ Monitoring and measurement – Customer satisfaction, Internal audits, Monitoring and measurement of processes, Monitoring and measurement of product
- ➤ Control of nonconforming product
- ➤ Analysis of data
- ➤ Improvement – Continual improvement, Corrective action, Preventive action

By comparing the ISO 9001:2000 version with the current version of ISO 9001, it is apparent that the major new requirements include Customer focus, Internal communication, Measurement and monitoring, Customer satisfaction, and Continual improvement. In other words, the company management must be actively involved in making the quality system work. The measurements and monitoring effectiveness of internal audits and corrective actions, monitoring of processes, and monitoring of products will reinforce the weakness in the current implementation of ISO requirements.

Simple Implementation Steps

➢ Understand the intent of the new standard.
➢ Identify processes required in your organization.
➢ Understand the process approach.
➢ Develop a business process map.
➢ Understand the difference between the current quality system and new version requirements.
➢ Develop a plan to utilize current elements and re-organize them in the new quality management system.
➢ Develop documents and implement them for new requirements.
➢ Revise current documentation and data collection methods for existing elements.
➢ Provide necessary training, explaining to all employees the significance of the new standard.
➢ Plan to realize benefits and demonstrate it.
➢ Make the new version work better for your organization than the previous one did.

The challenge for registrars is to be more focused on the intent of the standard requirements rather than literal compliance to the requirement. Training less experienced auditors in reviewing processes more for effectiveness rather than compliance will be a necessity. Without such an effort, the new ISO 9001:2000 requirements will be quite difficult to verify for compliance. In absence of such evidence, the registration auditors will be compromising the quality of audits. The organization's management will get the message that the requirements must not be important. Therefore, the significance of the ISO 9000 standard will be trivialized again and perceived as a lot of paperwork.

Consultants will have a challenge: they can no longer promise a client to get certified in 'three months' as some consultants had recommended. ISO 9001:2000 really requires that the quality system must evolve in the organization. A quality system is more than procedures and documentation. It is really implementation by employees for improving the profitability of the company. Certifying or re-certifying companies in three months without changing the mindset, culture or practices of the company, when needed, is a disservice to the ISO 9001:2000 standard as well as to society. Mere certification really causes a lot of waste in society.

The Registrar Accreditation Board (RAB) or equivalent bodies must also consider revising their auditor training programs. The current Lead Auditor training programs really focus on the compliance aspect of the standards much more than on the effectiveness of the quality system. The Lead Auditor trainees, ideally the organization's quality manager or management representative, currently return to their companies with the understanding of how to prepare to pass the audit using a checklist (more like a financial audit rather than a quality audit). Similarly, at the highest level, the ISO organization must also clearly communicate its policy or vision regarding the use of ISO 9001:2000 worldwide to realize its full potential.

The challenge for organizations that are already ISO 9001/2 registered is getting used to implementing the quality management system as it was intended. If the companies are utilizing their quality system effectively and realizing benefits in terms of quality improvement and profitability, the impact of ISO 9001:2000 will be minimal. However, if the companies are merely trying to maintain the certification with minimal effort, the challenge will be to change management's mindset.

Management (CEO or President) must accept the fact that the quality system is not a quality department's activity. Instead, the quality system is a chief executive's tool to manage business for growth and profitability. The management must understand that the quality system addresses all aspects of business operations except finance. However, if the operations are not managed as intended in the ISO 9001 standard, the chances of profitability are already quite slim.

ISO 9001:2000 must be supported with commitment from ISO, Accreditation Bodies, Registrars, Auditors and Management Representatives in order to implement the quality system in a 'quality' way and to justify its continuing success and the investment that organizations make in implementing the quality management system. In any case, the management has two choices: either profit from the implementation of the improved quality system as intended in a value-added manner, or suffer from its daily intricacies due to waste in the system.

ISO 9001:2000 Checklist

Guidelines for using the checklist

The ISO 9001:2000 checklist is designed to help organizations understand requirements and assess their quality system against the new requirements. The checklist can include 'Yes' or 'No' type questions or include open-ended questions. Since the purpose of the checklist is to really understand and assess the level of compliance and identify areas for improvement, the checklist contains open-ended statements. The open-ended question format allows for flexibility and application to various industries and circumstances, and for relative estimated rankings to establish a numerical benchmark. The numerical benchmark is an estimated level of implementation of the requirements that can be updated after corrective actions are implemented.

The checklist is divided according to the 1st (requirements 4 through 8) and 2nd (example: 4.1, 4.2...) level of requirements of the ISO 9001:2000 standard. Questions are numbered hierarchically, so each question can be traced to the corresponding requirement. This format also gives confidence to the auditor in the completeness of the assessment. Each question includes a note to clarify the requirement, or its assessment, from a business perspective. Sometimes it is difficult to clarify a simple statement about the requirement; however, an attempt has been made to clarify its assessment.

The ISO 9001:2000 has been revised to bring it in harmony with ISO 14001 and to address business feedback and increase the value of the quality system. As a result, sometimes some statements or requirements appear to be repeated. One must look at the requirement in the right context, in order to assess its' compliance. Where it appears to the author that the requirement has been addressed somewhere else, he has removed it. However, the checklist covers all requirements of the standard and utilizes field experience to interpret and clarify the requirements for implementation and assessment.

There are three components to be considered to score compliance. Each component is rated on a scale of 1 to 5. The three components are as follows:

Documentation	=>	D
Compliance	=>	C
Effectiveness	=>	E

To assess the degree of documentation, one must look into the approach to do a task, documentation methodology, and determining the level of institutionalization. To assess the level of compliance, one must look at the extent of implementation of the documented quality system. To assess effectiveness, one must look into the degree of product conformance (satisfactory functionality) or process performance (set up, monitor, controls, % level of acceptable output and consistency of results). The following table summarizes scoring guidelines:

To assess compliance using the checklist, one needs to become familiar with the intent of the question, scoring guidelines and auditing techniques. The checklist is divided among sections. The auditor can pick one section at a time;

review the checklist; and then use good interviewing skills to understand the informal system in practice.

Scoring Guidelines

Rating	Documentation (D)	Compliance (C)	Effectiveness (E)
(0-20) No formal approach	Adhoc documentation	No awareness of compliance to quality management processes	Adhoc relationship between documents and product realization
(21–40) Reactive approach	Documentation as needed	Some awareness and sporadic compliance to quality management processes	Effectiveness of quality management processes is not assessed regularly
(41-60) Stable formal system approach	Document control exists (Current ISO 9000 compliant documentation system)	Significant level of compliance to quality management processes	Effectiveness of quality management processes and product realization exists and evidence is present
(61-80) Continual improvement emphasized	Documents are simple to use and produce desired results	Full compliance and continual updating of documents	Effectiveness of the entire quality management system is evident and quality objectives are achieved.
(81-100) Best-in-class performance	Documentation is on-line, easy to access, utilized by employees frequently, and changed quickly to reflect changes	Full compliance, continual update, highly effective documents	High customer satisfaction, continual quality improvement is evident, quality objectives are exceeded

While listening to the auditee responses, the auditor must ask for evidence and review enough samples to gain confidence in assessing the level of documentation, compliance and effectiveness. Once the level of documentation, compliance and effectiveness are understood, a rating is assigned to each question. At the end of each section or after the completion of the audit, overall compliance ratings are determined and reported, along with necessary corrective actions.

ISO 9001:2000 Checklist

ISO 9001:2000 Self-Assessment Checklist

Q. #	Checklist Item (Notes)	D	C	E	Avg.	Comments
4.1	**Quality Management System – General Requirements**					
41Q1.1	Your company has established, documented, implemented and maintained a quality management system. *(Do you have a documented quality system that is compliant to the ISO 9001:2000 standard?)*					
41Q2.2	Your company has identified processes and their interaction needed for the quality management system. *(Do you have a current business process flowchart identifying various processes, including sales, engineering, operations, quality, management, calibration, customer service, technical support, etc.?)*					
41Q3.3	For the processes identified, your company has implemented procedures and controls to ensure effectiveness. *(Has your company documented good procedures and identified critical business process parameters and expected performance levels?)*					
41Q4.4	Your company provides enough resources to support the operation and monitoring of these processes. *(Does your company provide resources in terms of equipment, supplies, information, corrective actions, and employees' time for monitoring operations?)*					

ISO 9001:2000 Self-Assessment Checklist

Q. #	Checklist Item (Notes)	D	C	E	Avg.	Comments
41Q5.5	Your company analyzes process performance data, identifies opportunities for improvement and takes necessary actions for continual improvement. *(Is there a formal approach/system in place to analyze data? Are there reports published about process performance or the company's performance? Do you take actions based on the reports? Do you see improvement? If no improvement is seen, are actions taken to drive improvement?)*					
41Q6.6	Your company has included outsourced processes or service providers in the scope of supplier management procedures. *(Do you qualify and monitor outsourced processes or subcontractors?)*					

ISO 9001:2000 Self-Assessment Checklist

Q. #	Checklist Item (Notes)	D	C	E	Avg.	Comments
4.2	**Quality Management System – Documentation Requirements**					
42 Q1.7	Your quality system documentation includes a quality policy and objectives, quality manual, documented procedures, forms, necessary documents of external origin, etc. *(If all of the elements of the quality system are included in the documentation, it is great. If not, rate your quality system as appropriate based on the extent of the documentation.)*					
42 Q2.8	Your quality manual defines the scope/applicability of the quality management system, including any exclusion of the ISO 9001:2000 requirements, product lines, plants, processes, etc. *(Does your quality manual clearly define processes included in the quality management system?)*					
42 Q3.9	Your quality manual makes references to documented procedures. *(Does your quality manual reference the documented procedures, work instructions or other methods of doing the work?)*					
42 Q4.10	In your quality manual, various business processes (or standard elements) are connected by linking inputs and outputs of processes. *(In other words, how does one process' output go to the next process' input?)*					
42 Q5.11	Your document control procedures include review and approval of new or revised documents for adequacy. *(Are you ensuring that documents or changes are reviewed effectively by appropriate people for completeness and the ability to produce desired results?)*					

ISO 9001:2000 Self-Assessment Checklist

Q. #	Checklist Item (Notes)	D	C	E	Avg.	Comments
42 Q6.12	Your document control procedures include approval of new or revised documents prior to release. *(Do you have records of review and approval for evidence?)*					
42 Q7.13	Your document control procedures identify changes to documents and revision status. *(Do you track changes and version updates in your document control system?)*					
42 Q8.14	Your document control procedures ensure that relevant versions of documents are available at point of use and are legible (not soiled or unreadable), and obsolete documents are prevented from unintended use. *(You should be able to demonstrate that the user of documents can easily retrieve documents in much less time than it takes to perform the task. How do you ensure that old documents or versions are not available at point of use or prevent them from being used?)*					
42 Q9.15	Your documentation control procedures include identification and distribution of documents of external origin. *(Have you set up a master list, catalog or equivalent system to track availability of applicable documents of external origin? How do you ensure that the latest version of documents of external origin is available?)*					
42 Q10.16	Your document control procedures include identification of obsolete documents that are retained for any purpose. *(Do you keep a list of documents to be preserved for legal purposes?)*					

ISO 9001:2000 Self-Assessment Checklist

Q. #	Checklist Item (Notes)	D	C	E	Avg.	Comments
42 Q11.17	Your document control procedures require identification of records to be established for demonstration of conformity to requirements and the effective operation of processes of the quality management system. *(Have you created a log sheet, or required the creation of records for applicable processes, to ensure that the processes (when performed according to your procedures) produce desired results?)*					
42 Q12.18	Your quality records are legible, readily identifiable and retrievable. *(Are quality records neatly completed and retrievable for verification?)*					
42 Q13.19	Your company has established procedures for the identification, storage, protection, retrieval, retention time and disposition of quality records.					

ISO 9001:2000 Self-Assessment Checklist

Q. #	Checklist Item (Notes)	D	C	E	Avg.	Comments
5.1	**Management Responsibility – Management Commitment**					
51 Q1.20	Top management communicates to the organization its commitment to the quality system as well as the importance of meeting customer, statutory and regulatory requirements. *(What is the mechanism your management uses to communicate significance of compliance to quality management system requirements and compliance to OSHA, FDA, FAA, EPA, etc.? Examples are monthly meetings, periodical reminders, small group meetings, etc.).*					
51 Q2.21	Top management has established the quality policy and quality objectives. *(The relevant quality policy and related business quality objectives have been established and implemented.)*					
51 Q3.22	Top management conducts management reviews. *(Is your top management actively involved in planning and formally conducting management reviews according to documented procedures?)*					
51 Q4.23	Top management ensures adequate resources are available for activities affecting the quality of products or services to customers. *(Does your management regularly review resource requirements to ensure delivery of quality products and services to customers, and does your management provide necessary resources? Does evidence exist of such reviews?)*					

ISO 9001:2000 Self-Assessment Checklist

Q. #	Checklist Item (Notes)	D	C	E	Avg.	Comments

| 5.2 | **Management Responsibility – Customer Focus** | | | | | |
| 52 Q1.24 | Top management ensures that customer requirements are determined and focuses on improving customer satisfaction. *(Does your management review major customer expectations, meet with customers to understand expected requirements and capture their feedback?)* | | | | | |

ISO 9001:2000 Self-Assessment Checklist

Q. #	Checklist Item (Notes)	D	C	E	Avg.	Comments
5.3	**Management Responsibility – Quality Policy**					
53 Q1.25	Top management ensures that the quality policy is relevant to the purpose of your company. *(Top management participates in developing the company policy (vision), keeps it customer-focused and strives for internal quality improvement.)*					
53 Q2.26	Top management ensures that everyone understands the importance of being committed to comply with requirements and continual improvement of the quality management system. *(Company management communicates its commitment to requirements and continual improvement of the quality system to all employees regularly.)*					
53 Q3.27	Top management ensures that the quality policy is used as a framework for achieving quality objectives. *(The management utilizes the quality management system to realize the company's quality policy and business objectives.)*					
53 Q4.28	Top management ensures that the quality policy is communicated and understood by all employees within the company. *(The top management organizes meetings or creates opportunities for interaction with employees to discuss the quality policy, business objectives, and the company's quality performance.)*					

ISO 9001:2000 Self-Assessment Checklist

Q. #	Checklist Item (Notes)	D	C	E	Avg.	Comments
5.4	**Management Responsibility – Planning**					
54 Q1.29	Top management ensures that objective measurements for business, products and processes are established at various functions within your company. *(Top management has ensured that processes are mapped, inputs and outputs analysis is completed, and necessary controls have been defined and implemented.)*					
54 Q2.30	Top management ensures that planning for effectively implementing the quality management system is carried out. *(Top management utilizes management reviews and a formal quality planning process to ensure that the quality management system is implemented effectively.)*					
54 Q3.31	Top management ensures that the integrity of the quality management system is maintained when changes are made in the system. *(When changes are made, the quality management system is reviewed thoroughly for system completeness.)*					

ISO 9001:2000 Self-Assessment Checklist

Q. #	Checklist Item (Notes)	D	C	E	Avg.	Comments
5.5	**Management Responsibility – Responsibility, Authority and Communication**					
55 Q1.32	Top management ensures that responsibility and authority of personnel affecting quality are defined and communicated within your company. (Top management documents the quality-related responsibilities and authority of personnel using a matrix and then communicates this responsibility and authority to the appropriate employees via meetings, training, etc.)					
55 Q2.33	Top management shall designate an executive as the management representative for your company.					
55 Q3.34	Your management representative ensures that the quality management system is established, implemented and maintained.					
55 Q4.35	Your management representative reports to the management on the performance of the quality system and opportunities for improvement. *(Your management representative prepares a quality report for business performance measurements and presents audit findings for use in strengthening the company.)*					
55 Q5.36	Top management establishes a process for communicating effectiveness of the quality system along with other business-related issues. *(Are there some methods to communicate customer's needs/expectations to all employees?)*					

ISO 9001:2000 Self-Assessment Checklist

Q. #	Checklist Item (Notes)	D	C	E	Avg.	Comments
5.6	**Management Responsibility – Management Review**					
56 Q1.37	Your top management reviews performance of the quality system periodically to ensure its continuing suitability, adequacy and effectiveness. *(During the management review, the quality management system is reviewed for its applicability, completeness and desired results.)*					
56 Q2.38	The management review includes assessing opportunities for improvement and changes in the quality management system, including the quality policy.					
56 Q3.39	Records of management reviews are maintained for a specified time. *(Is there a clear method and place for filing records of management review meetings?)*					
56 Q4.40	During the management review, audit results, customer feedback, process performance and product conformance, status of corrective and preventive actions, status of action items from the previous meeting, potential changes to the quality management system, and opportunities for improvement are reviewed. *(Is there an agenda to ensure all the items are consistently reviewed in each meeting?*					
56 Q5.41	The management review report includes actions or decisions related to improvement of the effectiveness of the quality management system, product improvement, and needed resources. *(Is the report complete, and does it include all the items from the agenda for the management review meeting?)*					

ISO 9001:2000 Self-Assessment Checklist

Q. #	Checklist Item (Notes)	D	C	E	Avg.	Comments
6.1	**Resource Management – Provision of Resources**					
61 Q1.42	Your company assesses and provides necessary resources to maintain and improve the quality system effectively. *(Are there records of reviewing the company's resource requirements and the provision of such resources, or are alternative plans developed?)*					
61 Q2.43	Your company determines and provides necessary resources to improve customer satisfaction. *(Company has plans, procedures and necessary resources to understand customer needs and improve customer satisfaction.)*					

ISO 9001:2000 Self-Assessment Checklist

Q. #	Checklist Item (Notes)	D	C	E	Avg.	Comments
6.2	**Resource Management – Human Resources**					
62 Q1.44	Employees performing work affecting quality are qualified based on education, training, skills and experience. *(Employees are recruited or assigned tasks based on their capability.)*					
62 Q2.45	Your company determines the competence required for personnel performing work affecting quality.					
62 Q3.46	Your company provides necessary training to ensure qualified personnel perform the work affecting quality. *(Training procedures and records will give evidence of a plan for training and provision of training.*					
62 Q4.47	Your company evaluates effectiveness of the training effort to improve personnel competence. *(Some effort and evidence. e.g., performance appraisals, testing, etc., exists to evaluate effectiveness of training based on the achievement of business objectives.)*					
62 Q5.48	Your company ensures that personnel understand the importance and relevance of their work in achieving quality objectives. *(Company management communicates benefits of achieving quality objectives and consequences of not achieving quality..)*					
62 Q6.49	Your company maintains appropriate records of education, training, skills and experience. *(Your company has documented job descriptions for various positions, including required competence, and records are maintained.)*					

ISO 9001:2000 Self-Assessment Checklist

Q. #	Checklist Item (Notes)	D	C	E	Avg.	Comments
6.3	**Resource Management – Infrastructure**					
63 Q1.50	Your company determines and provides necessary facilities, process equipment, tools, software, and supporting services (e.g., transport and communication). *(Does your company management ensure that appropriate equipment, material, methods and people are available for producing products or services?)*					

Q. #	Checklist Item (Notes)	D	C	E	Avg.	Comments
6.4	**Resource Management – Work Environment**					
64 Q1.51	Your company maintains a suitable work environment to ensure conformity to product requirements. *(A suitable work environment is ensured in the production area, laboratories, customer service area, technical support area, storage, etc.)*					

ISO 9001:2000 Self-Assessment Checklist

Q. #	Checklist Item (Notes)	D	C	E	Avg.	Comments
7.1	**Product Realization – Planning of Product Realization**					
71 Q1.52	Your company plans and develops processes to realize product or services. *(The company has a documented plan or the equivalent to produce the product.)*					
71 Q2.53	The product (product, project or service) realization plan is compatible with other requirements of the quality management system. *(Your product realization plan does not conflict with the quality management system requirements.)*					
71 Q3.54	In planning for the processes needed for product realization, your company determines, as appropriate, quality objectives and requirements for the product, resources for establishing processes and documents, process control activities (verification, validation, testing, monitoring, inspection), and necessary records to verify that the realization processes and resulting product meet requirements. *(A product realization flow chart, with appropriate steps, is documented and implemented.)*					
71 Q4.55	The product realization plan is effectively implemented. *(Does the product realization plan enable the company to produce products/services that meet or exceed customer expectations?)*					

ISO 9001:2000 Self-Assessment Checklist

Q. #	Checklist Item (Notes)	D	C	E	Avg.	Comments
7.2	**Product Realization – Customer-related Processes**					
72 Q1.56	Your company determines customer requirements, including delivery and after delivery activities. *(The customer contract review process exists for documenting delivery and service requirements.)*					
72 Q2.57	The customer requirements include implied needs as well as statutory, regulatory, and additional necessary requirements. *(The sales process ensures various types of requirements are examined for completeness of customer requirements.)*					
72 Q3.58	Your company reviews product/ service requirements prior to commitment to supply a product. *(Customer requirements are reviewed and authorized by appropriate personnel prior to release.)*					
72 Q4.59	Your company ensures that product requirements are defined, conflicting requirements are resolved, and defined require-ments can be met. *(Before starting product realization, customer requirements are understood, including changes or trade-off.)*					
72 Q5.60	Records of the review results and related actions are maintained. *(A filing system for customer requirements, e.g., contracts, amendments, notes, communication records exists.)*					

ISO 9001:2000 Self-Assessment Checklist

Q. #	Checklist Item (Notes)	D	C	E	Avg.	Comments
72 Q6.61	In the absence of documented customer requirements, your company confirms requirements before acceptance. *(When customer requirements have not been documented, a confirmation of customer requirements for implicit agreement must be in place.)*					
72 Q7.62	Changes in product requirements or customer requirements are reflected in appropriate documents and communicated to relevant personnel. *(Changes in customer requirements are accepted internally prior to accepting with the customer. Changes in customer requirements are understood, documented, and communicated in a timely manner to appropriate functions.)*					
72 Q8.63	Your company establishes effective arrangements for communicating with the customer regarding product information, inquiries, sales, order handling and customer feedback, including customer complaints. *(A well-established method to communicate customer requirements exists.)*					

ISO 9001:2000 Self-Assessment Checklist

Q. #	Checklist Item (Notes)	D	C	E	Avg.	Comments
7.3	**Product Realization – Design and Development**					
73 Q1.64	Your company plans and controls the design and development of product. *(Product design and development methodology or procedures exists.)*					
73 Q2.65	The design and development plan includes design and development stages, including review, verification and validation of design and development. *(The design and development plan is comprehensive and complete with measurable milestones.)*					
73 Q3.66	The design and development plan includes interfaces, clear responsibilities and authorities for design and development. *(The design and development plan identifies names, functions, and expected deliverables.)*					
73 Q4.67	The design and development plan is reviewed for progress and updated as appropriate. *(The design and development progress is reviewed against the plan, and the plan is updated appropriately.)*					
73 Q5.68	Records of input to the design and development plan are maintained. *(Input to the design and development process is identified, and records are maintained to ensure effective implementation.)*					

ISO 9001:2000 Self-Assessment Checklist

Q. #	Checklist Item (Notes)	D	C	E	Avg.	Comments
73 Q6.69	Input to the design and development plan includes functional and performance requirements, statutory and regulatory requirements and lessons from the history of similar designs. *(The requirements consist of functional, physical, environmental, statutory, regulatory and other expectations.)*					
73 Q7.70	The input is reviewed for adequacy, completeness, and trade-off. *(A preliminary review of input is conducted according to the plan, thus ensuring the adequacy of design requirements.)*					
73 Q8.71	The design and development output enables verification against the design and development input. *(The design and development output is such that a relationship between input and output can be established for traceability and completeness of design.)*					
73 Q9.72	The design and development output is approved prior to release. *(Design and development documents, e.g., prints, instructions, and acceptability standards, are reviewed and approved prior to releasing for further processing or production.)*					
73 Q10.73	The design and development output meets input requirements for design and development and provides information for purchasing, production and service. *(The design and development output is communicated to appropriate functions for necessary actions.)*					

ISO 9001:2000 Self-Assessment Checklist

Q. #	Checklist Item (Notes)	D	C	E	Avg.	Comments
73 Q11.74	The design and development output contains reference to product acceptance criteria. *(Workmanship standards, test plans, and final inspection, etc. have been identified in the design and development output.)*					
73 Q12.75	The design and development output specifies essential product characteristics for safe and proper operation. *(Critical product characteristics, and their control, are identified for field performance of the product.)*					
73 Q13.76	Design and development reviews, according to documented procedures, are conducted at suitable stages according to the design and development plan. *(Reviews are conducted at appropriate design and development stages as per the design plan.)*					
73 Q14.77	The design and development reviews include examining the ability to meet requirements, identify problems and take necessary actions. *(Records of reviews include critical issues, corresponding actions, responsibilities and schedules.)*					
73 Q15.78	The design and development reviews include participation from relevant functions. *(Personnel from departments concerned with design and development participate in these reviews.)*					
73 Q16.79	Records of design and development reviews, including appropriate actions, are maintained. *(A method to maintain design and development review records is effectively implemented.)*					

ISO 9001:2000 Self-Assessment Checklist

Q. #	Checklist Item (Notes)	D	C	E	Avg.	Comments
73 Q17.80	Design and development verification of outputs against input requirements is performed, and records are maintained. *(The relationship between design and development inputs and outputs is established and documented.)*					
73 Q18.81	Design and development validation is performed as per the design plan to ensure that it meets the intended use or the requirements prior to delivery or implementation of the product. *(Validation of design and development against the requirements and intended use is performed at appropriate stages.)*					
73 Q19.82	Records of design and development validation and necessary actions are maintained. *(A method to maintain records of design and development validation has been established and effectively implemented.)*					
73 Q20.83	Design and development changes are identified and maintained. *(Design and development change control procedures have been established and implemented.)*					
73 Q21.84	The design and development changes are reviewed, verified, validated, and approved prior to implementation. *(The design and development changes are reviewed and authorized by relevant area managers for implementation.)*					
73 Q22.85	Records of review of the design and development changes and necessary actions are maintained. *(Methods, or a database to maintain design changes for traceability and product history, exist.)*					

ISO 9001:2000 Self-Assessment Checklist

Q. #	Checklist Item (Notes)	D	C	E	Avg.	Comments
7.4	**Product Realization – Purchasing**					
74 Q1.86	Your organization ensures that purchased product conforms to your purchase requirements. *(A process to specify purchasing requirements is clearly defined, understood and documented.)*					
74 Q2.87	Your company has established appropriate control over supplier and the purchased product based on the effect of the purchased product throughout the product realization process. *(Suppliers' capability, product performance records and field performance are reviewed, and necessary controls are established, to ensure acceptability of the purchased product.)*					
74 Q3.88	Your company evaluates suppliers for their ability to meet your business requirements. *(A supplier's evaluation process is implemented effectively.)*					
74 Q4.89	Criteria for supplier selection, evaluation, monitoring and re-evaluation are established. *(A supplier management process is defined and documented to initially qualify, and then monitor, suppliers' performance for on-going qualification, supplier development and improvement.)*					

ISO 9001:2000 Self-Assessment Checklist

Q. #	Checklist Item (Notes)	D	C	E	Avg.	Comments
74 Q5.90	Records of suppliers' performance during evaluation and after approval are maintained. *(Methods for keeping suppliers' performance records are documented and effectively implemented.)*					
74 Q6.91	Purchasing requirements include, where appropriate, approval requirements for product, procedures, processes and equipment. *(Purchasing documents specify, when necessary, approval or conformance certification requirements.)*					
74 Q7.92	Purchasing requirements also include quality management system requirements and qualification of personnel. *(Purchasing documents specify quality management system, acceptance, and personnel qualification requirements for the completion/product realization.)*					
74 Q8.93	Your company ensures that purchase requirements are reviewed for adequacy prior to communication to the supplier. *(Evidence of review and authorization of purchase orders prior to release exists.)*					
74 Q9.94	For verification of purchased product at the supplier's location, including verification by your customers, your purchasing requirements include the intended verification arrangements and method of product release. *(Purchasing requirements include necessary verifications.)*					

ISO 9001:2000 Self-Assessment Checklist

Q. #	Checklist Item (Notes)	D	C	E	Avg.	Comments
7.5	**Product Realization –** **Production and Service Provision**					
75 Q1.95	Your company plans and controls production of product or service under controlled conditions. *(The production plan, schedule, acquisition of necessary resources and release of product are performed in a systematic way.)*					
75 Q2.96	Controlled conditions for provision of product and services include product requirements and the use of suitable equipment. *(All necessary material, methods, machines, people, environmental conditions and measurement devices are available for production purposes.)*					
75 Q3.97	Controlled conditions for provision of product and services also include the use of monitoring and measuring devices and methods. *(Monitoring and measuring devices include calibrated inspection, measuring and test equipment, process control, data collection and analysis methods.)*					
75 Q4.98	The plan to carry out provision of product and services also includes implementation of release, delivery and post-delivery activities. *(The production plans include processes, packaging, storage, shipping, preservation and delivery to the customer.)*					
75 Q5.99	Your company validates processes for production and service where process output cannot be verified subsequently. *(For special processes, effective process controls are implemented.)*					

ISO 9001:2000 Self-Assessment Checklist

Q. #	Checklist Item (Notes)	D	C	E	Avg.	Comments
75 Q6.100	Validation of such processes includes criteria for applicable review and approval of processes, equipment, qualification of personnel, specific methods and procedures, requirements for records and revalidation. *(Sufficient controls of special processes to ensure required process capability are implemented.)*					
75 Q7.101	Where appropriate, your company has established suitable means to identify product and product status throughout product realization. *(Throughout operations, product and its status is identified appropriately using tags, stickers, work orders, or other appropriate means.)*					
75 Q9.102	When required, your company controls and maintains records of unique identification of the product. *(Methods to maintain product identification records have been established.)*					
75 Q10.10 3	Your company identifies, verifies, protects and safeguards customer property, including intellectual property, tools, material or equipment.					
75 Q11.10 4	Your company maintains records and notifies the customer of property that is lost, damaged or unsuitable for use. *(Methods to handle lost or damaged customer-supplied material have been established and implemented.)*					
75 Q12.10 5	Your company preserves (handling, packaging, storage and protection) the conformity of product or constituent parts during internal processing and delivery to the intended destination.					

ISO 9001:2000 Self-Assessment Checklist

Q. #	Checklist Item (Notes)	D	C	E	Avg.	Comments
7.6	**Product Realization – Control of Monitoring and Measuring Devices**					
76 Q1.106	Your company determines measurements and measuring devices needed to ensure product conformity to specified requirements. *(Appropriate measurements and measuring devices at various stages during operations have been identified.)*					
76 Q2.107	Your company has established a process to ensure effective monitoring and measurement of required processes. *(Work orders, control plans or equivalent methods have been implemented to ensure required measurements are taken and data are collected.)*					
76 Q3.108	Where necessary, the measuring equipment are calibrated or verified at specified intervals, or prior to use, against measurement standards. *(Accuracy and precision of measuring devices is ensured through calibration or verification processes.)*					
76 Q4.109	Measurement standards are traceable to national or international standards, or the basis used for calibration or verification is recorded. *(Master measurement devices are calibrated against and traceable to national and international standards.)*					
76 Q5.110	Measurement equipment are identified with the calibration status. *(Stickers or labels showing calibration or verification status are utilized to prevent use of inaccurate measurement devices.)*					

ISO 9001:2000 Self-Assessment Checklist

Q. #	Checklist Item (Notes)	D	C	E	Avg.	Comments
76 Q6.111	Measurement equipment are safeguarded from any adjustments that would invalidate results. (*Measurement devices are stored in a limited access area to prevent unauthorized adjustment.*)					
76 Q7.112	Measurement equipment is protected from damage or deterioration during handling, maintenance and storage. (*Proper handling, storage and environmental practices are utilized to prevent damage.*)					
76 Q8.113	When equipment is found to be nonconforming, the validity of previous measurements is assessed and recorded. (*Impact of using out-of-tolerance equipment is assessed for identification of potential recall.*)					
76 Q9.114	Your company takes appropriate action on the equipment or product affected by the invalid measurements.					
76 Q10.115	Records of calibration and verification activities are maintained. (*Methods for maintaining calibration and verification records have been defined and implemented.*)					
76 Q11.116	When software is used in the monitoring and measurement of specified requirements, the software is confirmed to satisfy the intended application prior to initial use and re-checked as necessary. (*Measurement devices or constituents that cannot be calibrated must be checked and re-checked at prescribed intervals.*)					

ISO 9001:2000 Self-Assessment Checklist

Q. #	Checklist Item (Notes)	D	C	E	Avg.	Comments
8.1	**Measurement, Analysis and Improvement – General**					
81 Q1.117	Your company plans and implements monitoring, measurement, and analysis to demonstrate conformity of the product and conformity of the quality management system. *(Data collection and analysis methods have been defined, documented and implemented to ensure conformity and identification of opportunities for improvement.)*					
81 Q2.118	Your company continually improves the effectiveness of the quality management system. *(Company management has communicated its philosophy, demonstrated its commitment, and implemented action plans to improve the quality management system.)*					
81 Q3.119	Your company determines applicable statistical techniques and the extent of their use. *(Company has, where practical, identified and utilized statistical techniques for data analysis.)*					

ISO 9001:2000 Self-Assessment Checklist

Q. #	Checklist Item (Notes)	D	C	E	Avg.	Comments
8.2	**Measurement, Analysis and Improvement – Monitoring and Measurement**					
82 Q1.120	Your company has established a method to monitor customer satisfaction. *(A perceived and stated customer feedback/ satisfaction assessment process has been defined and implemented.)*					
82 Q2.121	Your company conducts internal quality audits to determine compliance and effectiveness of the quality management system against the documented procedures and the ISO 9001:2000 standard requirements. *(An internal quality audit program has been implemented to ensure compliance and effectiveness of the quality management system.)*					
82 Q3.122	The internal quality audits are planned considering the status and importance of the processes and the areas to be audited as well as the results of the previous audits. *(Internal audits are planned and scheduled based on process and product performance.)*					
82 Q4.123	The internal quality audit procedures include audit criteria, scope, frequency, methods, selection of auditors, and how to conduct audits. *(Internal audit procedures adequately document the internal audit process for effective implementation.)*					
82 Q5.124	The internal quality auditors are independent of the area(s) they audit, thus ensuring objectivity. *(Objectivity of audits is maintained through scheduling auditors independent of their functions.)*					

ISO 9001:2000 Self-Assessment Checklist

Q. #	Checklist Item (Notes)	D	C	E	Avg.	Comments
82 Q6.125	Responsibilities for planning, conducting, reporting and maintaining audit records are clearly defined in a documented procedure. *(The organization chart and corresponding documented procedure define responsibility for managing the internal audit program.)*					
82 Q7.126	The management of the area being audited ensures that timely corrective actions are taken to remedy nonconformance. *(Verifiable timely corrective actions are taken to prevent the recurrence of nonconformance.)*					
82 Q8.127	Follow-up audits are conducted to verify the reporting and effectiveness of corrective actions. *(Corrective actions are verified, or follow-up audits are done, for implementation and effectiveness.)*					
82 Q9.128	Your company reviews the effectiveness of the quality management processes to ensure planned results are achieved. *(Effectiveness of the quality management system is reviewed through analyzing the results achieved and compliance to the system.)*					
82 Q10.129	When a process does not produce desired results, appropriate corrective actions are taken to ensure conformity of the product. *(Records of appropriate corrective actions based on the data analysis are available.)*					

ISO 9001:2000 Self-Assessment Checklist

Q. #	Checklist Item (Notes)	D	C	E	Avg.	Comments
82 Q11.13 0	Your company monitors and measures product characteristics at appropriate stages to verify conformance to the specified requirements. *(The business flow chart identifying various processes and related measurements is available and implemented.)*					
82 Q12.13 1	Records of product conformity, with the acceptance criteria and the person(s) authorizing release of product, are maintained. *(Final inspection and release of the product for delivery are maintained according to defined methods.)*					
82 Q13.13 2	Release of product or service does not proceed unless it satisfactorily meets the planned arrangements for verification, or is authorized by relevant authority or the customer, when applicable. *(A final authority, including the customer, has been defined and implemented to ensure necessary processes have been completed and product conforms to customer requirements.)*					

ISO 9001:2000 Self-Assessment Checklist

Q. #	Checklist Item (Notes)	D	C	E	Avg.	Comments
8.3	**Measurement, Analysis and Improvement – Control of Nonconforming Material**					
83 Q1.133	Your company ensures that unacceptable product is identified and controlled to prevent its unintended use or delivery.					
83 Q2.134	Responsibilities and authorities for handling of nonconforming material are defined in a documented procedure. *(A process to handle nonconforming material has been documented and implemented effectively.)*					
83 Q3.135	Handling of the nonconforming product includes actions to eliminate the nonconformity or authorize its use, release or acceptance with deviation by a relevant authority, including the customer, when applicable, and actions to preclude its original intended use. *(Nonconforming material is prevented from release or delivery.)*					
83 Q4.136	Records of the nature of nonconformities and subsequent actions, including concessions obtained from the customer, are maintained. *(Methods for keeping records of handling nonconforming material and necessary actions have been defined and documented.)*					
83 Q5.137	Any repaired or reworked product is re-verified to demonstrate its conformity to the requirements. *(Repaired product is verified, and records are available, to ensure conformity to customer requirements.)*					

ISO 9001:2000 Self-Assessment Checklist

Q. #	Checklist Item (Notes)	D	C	E	Avg.	Comments
84 Q6.138	Your company takes action to remedy the effects of the nonconformity detected after delivery or use of product. (*Assessment of impact of delivering nonconforming product has been defined in case of positive recall.*)					

ISO 9001:2000 Self-Assessment Checklist

Q. #	Checklist Item (Notes)	D	C	E	Avg.	Comments
8.4	**Measurement, Analysis and Improvement – Analysis of Data**					
84 Q1.139	Your company determines, collects and analyzes data to demonstrate the suitability and effectiveness of the quality management system and identify opportunities for improvement. *(A method to analyze records, data collected and actions taken to determine suitability and effectiveness of the quality management system, and necessary changes to it, has been defined and implemented.)*					
84 Q2.140	The analysis of data provides information regarding customer satisfaction, conformity to product requirements, level and trends in processes, suppliers' performance and opportunities for preventive action. *(Data analysis includes levels, trends, and feedback to identify opportunities for improvement.)*					

ISO 9001:2000 Self-Assessment Checklist

Q. #	Checklist Item (Notes)	D	C	E	Avg.	Comments
8.5	**Measurement, Analysis and Improvement – Improvement**					
85 Q1.141	Your company continually improves the effectiveness of the quality management system through the use of the quality policy, quality objectives, audit results, analysis of data, corrective and preventive actions, and management review. *(Realization of the quality policy, objectives, and effectiveness of corrective actions is reviewed to determine effectiveness of the quality system.)*					
85 Q2.142	Your company takes corrective actions, appropriate to the effects of nonconformities, to eliminate the cause of nonconformities. *(Corrective actions are appropriately identified and effectively implemented.)*					
85 Q3.143	A documented procedure has been established to define requirements for reviewing nonconformities, determining root cause analysis and corrective action, implementing corrective action, recording action taken, and reviewing effectiveness of corrective action taken. *(A corrective action process has been documented and implemented. Emphasis is placed on verification and the closed-loop process.)*					
85 Q4.144	Your company identifies appropriate preventive actions to prevent the cause of potential nonconformities. *(Using trends, customer feedback, and quality objectives, actions are identified to prevent future nonconformities.)*					

ISO 9001:2000 Self-Assessment Checklist

Q. #	Checklist Item (Notes)	D	C	E	Avg.	Comments
85 Q5.145	A documented procedure has been established to define requirements for determining potential nonconformities, evaluating the need for preventive action, implementing preventive action, recording action taken, and reviewing the effectiveness of preventive action. *(Preventive action or process improvement methodology has been defined, documented and implemented.)*					

Conducting Good Internal Audits

Introduction

The implementation of quality systems worldwide, such as ISO 9000, has lead to the deployment of supposedly sound management practices for more than 300,000 companies. However, the implementation of quality systems for many registered companies is questionable. Some of the problems these companies are having stem from the following beliefs and/or concerns:

➢ Our system does not need improvement; we just want the certificate.
➢ The Quality Department is responsible for quality.
➢ We do not have time for quality, so we have hired a consultant.
➢ Now that our company is certified, what do we do with our quality system?

Whether or not a company is seeking ISO 9000 certification, compliance to another quality system or just a good management system, internal audits should be conducted to ensure that processes are being done correctly and effectively for the company. The internal audit is not a new process that has been invented for ISO 9000 quality systems. The military has been doing quality audits, and accounting firms have been doing financial audits (i.e., examining accounting records to ensure appropriate reporting) for years.

ISO requires audits to be conducted to "verify whether quality activities and related results comply with planned arrangements and to determine the effectiveness of the system." If a company was going to ensure appropriate reporting of its accounting records by doing financial audits, why would the company not perform internal audits to ensure quality products are being produced? Without good quality products or services, a company's financial records may be compliant to the accounting practices and regulations, but the company will not be a profitable business. So whether or not a company is seeking ISO 9000 certification, a good management system involves setting up company goals, designing processes to meet those goals and reviewing actions to ensure that the defined goals are being met. So how does a company successfully perform audits of its system?

Setting Up a Value Added Internal Audit System

The first step is to plan and document the audit process by clearly identifying key steps, including the following:

- Audit planning
- Scheduling
- Implementing
- Reporting
- Taking corrective actions
- Verifying corrective actions
- Reviewing audits' value

Proper planning and communication of such plans helps ensure that audits are done correctly and consistently every time regardless of who is conducting the audit.

The intent of an internal audit is to ensure that the correct processes are in place and that they are being performed as planned. The results of the audit should identify what was found unacceptable (nonconforming) to the process or standard requirements. It is the auditor's responsibility to identify what is questionable in the process -- not the cause of the nonconforming condition or who made the mistake. Many companies do not clarify this intent clearly, and internal audits become a threat to employees instead of an opportunity to identify process improvements as intended.

Types of Audits

It is important to remember that one is not only auditing compliance to a procedure(s), but you are also auditing the guidelines and/or standards used to develop processes. Business goals change, technology changes, customer requirements change, and guidelines and standards change. Companies need to ensure that processes remain in compliance to applicable guidelines and standards in their industry. Companies must ensure that they have the best processes implemented to meet the requirements of their customers and the goals of the company.

A company can plan different types of audits at the same time or independently. A system audit is a verification of your entire quality system to ensure compliance to guideline and/or standard requirements (e.g., ISO 9000). The system audits are beneficial in order to periodically evaluate and re-apply various elements of the quality system. A process audit is an audit of a process against its documented procedures and/or quality plans in order to ensure compliance to requirements and effectiveness of the process. The process audits are useful in maintaining employees' awareness to the quality expectations and identifying opportunities for improvement.

Conducting the system audit at the same time you are conducting your process audits may save time for your company. However, when auditing both to the standard and the process, verification of effectiveness may be lost. In order to audit compliance to a standard, it usually involves many procedures, causing confusion and many missed areas. Additionally, one should audit all areas of the standard regardless if they are originally applicable to your company, because a company may have changed over time, now making that element relevant. Knowing what should be audited and how your company is managed, the auditors need to determine what process works best for the company and develop an audit system that best meets the company's needs.

Who Should Conduct Audits

Employees conduct internal audits, because they better understand the goals of the company and the organizational structure. A consultant may be hired to help train the employees or to demonstrate sample audits for a better understanding of the auditing process.

In order to conduct audits effectively, auditors should be qualified based on their interest, training and skills. Employees chosen to be auditors should be personable, well organized, objective, and have the ability to collect the information needed to determine compliance. Auditors also need to evaluate the information collected impartially to ensure that the perception of audits is positive for the company. Auditees who are not comfortable with their auditor will try to cover up the results of their processes, therefore making the identification of opportunities for improvement difficult.

Once trained, internal auditors should be assigned to audit areas independent of their responsibility. Independence eliminates bias from influencing audit results. Also, if an auditor is independent of the process being audited, he/she needs to question the process more just to understand it (in order to objectively audit the process). This questioning of the process triggers the auditee to consider a process in a different way he/she may have never considered, possibly identifying an opportunity to improve the process. A comprehensive auditing process consists of scheduling and preparing, conducting, reporting, taking corrective actions, following up and review by management.

Scheduling and Preparing for the Audit

An annual schedule should be developed identifying all the processes, guidelines and/or standards to be audited. This annual audit schedule should also specify frequency of these audits; who conducts the audit; and what department or area is to be audited.

All processes, guidelines and/or standards should be audited at least once a year. A company may decide that once a year is too much for some processes that are not likely to change. However, by auditing at least once a year, the process is at least reviewed to ensure that the guidelines and standards used to develop the process have not become obsolete.

How often an audit must occur should also be based on performance (status) and value (importance) of processes.

Obviously a company has some key processes that must be complied with to function effectively. These areas should be audited more than once a year. As for status, through previous audits, customer complaints and/or the internal rejects, problem processes can be identified. Processes with problems should be audited more often to help determine how best to improve the process and/or to ensure that changes made to improve the process are effective over time.

The auditor should contact the department(s) to be audited to ensure the time is convenient for them and that the right person or people is/are available to interact with the auditor through the process. It is important that the audit is scheduled for a time that is good for the auditor and the auditees so that audit results are based on objective evidence and not on conclusions derived from limited understanding.

An audit checklist should be developed to ensure that all requirements are identified and reviewed during the audit. This checklist should include internally defined process requirements, standard requirements, process needs, and the potential areas for improvement in terms of quality, productivity and cost.

Conducting the Audit

The audit process should begin with a discussion on what is going to take place during the audit so that the auditee clearly understands what will be expected of him/her. The auditor should use his/her checklist to guide the audit -- not use it as a check-off list. The auditor shall ensure that each requirement is reviewed for compliance and effectiveness of the process. The auditor should document the evidence that was reviewed during the audit and the results of his/her review directly on the checklist.

Once the audit is complete, the auditor should summarize the findings. By summarizing the findings at the end of the audit, the auditee has an opportunity to clarify any misunderstandings the auditor may have had. Such misunderstandings can result in the identification of incorrect nonconformance, which may further lead to unnecessary time spent researching problems that do not really exist.

Reporting Audits

Once the audit has been completed, the auditor should document his/her findings in a report. This report should identify the process and/or standard audited, the date of the audit, the name of the auditor, and observations made regarding conformance and nonconformances identified between process steps and procedures. The nonconformances should be specific as to what, where, and when so it is easier to research the cause of the problem in order to fix it.

The audit report should be submitted to the individuals audited, the manager of the department and executive management for review. The department manager should be responsible for correcting the nonconformances. He/she may assign other individuals to do the actual work, but as the department manager, he/she is responsible for the effective functioning of his/her department and continuous improvement. Upper management should use these reports to identify opportunities for improvement to eliminate potential nonconforming conditions, to assess company performance to established goals and to develop new goals as needed.

Taking Action on Nonconformance

Once a nonconformance has been identified, process management should investigate the root cause of the nonconforming condition. This is a difficult process for many companies, as the first reaction of managers is to seek an answer for "Who caused the problem?" Many employees do not understand the process of root cause analysis and therefore tend to remedy the symptom of the problem rather than determining its cause. This leads to recurrence of the problem and frustration.

Fish bone diagrams (Cause and Effect Analysis), or looking at machine (tools or equipment), material (information), mind (people) and method (procedures), is a good way to investigate the root cause of the problem. The following is a list of sample questions that may be asked during root cause analysis:

➢ Was the right equipment used?
➢ Was the equipment in proper working condition?
➢ Was the equipment operated correctly?
➢ Was the material to specification?
➢ Could better material be used?
➢ Was the process done correctly?
➢ Is the process effective or can it be done better?
➢ Are employees qualified?
➢ Were employees trained correctly?

A major problem companies experience in solving a nonconforming condition is to blame people first. However, employees should be considered last. There may be many possible causes of the problem. Management should place emphasis on the larger issues, because by eliminating the larger problems, the smaller ones are usually also addressed. Management must assume people want to do a good job and look for ways to help them in solving a problem.

It is important to note that the nonconformances must be communicated immediately. The management determines if the action needs to be taken immediately or at a later date. Managers must remember, though, that delay in remedying the nonconformances will only lead to more nonconforming products or services to customers. Many managers do overlook the addressing of nonconforming issues; that is why many managers spend more time putting out fires and do not have time for continuous improvement.

Following Up Corrective Actions

It is not enough to simply take action to address the nonconformance. Someone in the company should be assigned to review actions taken to eliminate nonconformances in order to ensure that the actions were actually implemented and that they were effective. An action item may have been to fix a machine, and it may have been fixed, but the problem may still be occurring. Action items need to be verified to determine if the correct action has eliminated the nonconformance.

Reviewing of Audit Results by Management

The above process of issuing corrective actions, performing root cause analysis and conducting follow up should all be documented. Maintaining a history of the corrective actions taken can save a lot of money in solving the same problem many times and can prevent making repeat mistakes.

The ISO 9000 standard notes that the results of internal quality audits are an integral part of the input to management review activities, but for many companies, what is meant by results is unclear. The audits should be completed as scheduled, so management should not be concerned with who has completed their audits and who has not. Management should be concerned with what was observed during the audit and what nonconforming issues were identified. These results (audits' degree of compliance, effectiveness and value) should be reviewed to determine necessary actions to improve the auditing process. The intent is the same as that of the auditors: continual improvement. If nonconforming issues are addressed in the management review, instead of employees the management identifies corrective actions. The ownership of the process is taken away from employees. Problems recur.

Conclusion

ISO 9000 was developed primarily for setting guidelines, including internal quality audits, for a company to follow to ensure customer requirements are met. So whether or not your company is seeking ISO 9000, internal audits are a great way to review processes to ensure they are being executed correctly and consistently. After all, customers prefer to work with companies that meet or exceed their needs. Without customers, a need is not there to be met. No business can succeed.

To maintain a competitive advantage, everyone must be responsible for quality and look for ways for the company to improve and differentiate themselves from the competition for greater customer satisfaction and value. In order to stay on top, it is better to do it right the first time than do it fast and redo it many times. Internal audits can help companies deliver good products on time, while reducing waste and improving profitability.

Beyond Quality - Implementing ISO 14001

During the last several months, more and more large corporations have been endorsing implementation of the ISO 14001 standard for their suppliers. An industry that is process-oriented can have a significant impact in reducing waste and improving awareness about environmental issues. The ISO 9001 and ISO 14001 standards are two sides of the same coin. The ISO 14001 standard is implemented to achieve excellence by reducing waste, while the ISO 9001 standard is implemented to reduce waste by achieving excellence.

Introduction

In the 1960s, environmental pollution was finally recognized as a social problem. The 1970s marked the birth of Earth Day, a nationally recognized day set aside for the purpose of increasing awareness of environmental issues and threats. In the 1980s, regulatory bodies like the Environmental Protection Agency (EPA) became active, recognizing industry's contributing role in environmental deterioration. Industries of the 1990s are taking a leadership role in the environmental management movement, with many companies investing large financial amounts for the purpose of furthering environmentally friendly policies, procedures and programs. Some of these programs include the following: design-for-the-environment engineering, waste minimization, pollution prevention, process changes, life-cycle analysis, energy and resource conservation, recycling, product stewardship and ISO 14001. The mentality of cradle-to-grave manufacturing has now become cradle-to-cradle manufacturing, as more and more companies are actively looking for creative ways to minimize waste and re-use or re-work their scrap.

The ISO 14001 standard has been released for more than two years. Its acceptance has been increasing steadily. More than six thousand companies have been certified to the ISO 14001 standards (Quality Digest, 12/98). Just like ISO 9000 standards, the US industry has been cautious in implementing the ISO 14001 standard. About 200 companies have been certified in the U.S. to ISO 14001. The supply chain pressure began to build when IBM and Ford announced their support for the implementation of ISO 14001 compliant environmental management systems.

The reasons for lingering acceptance of ISO 14001 include confusion caused by commonality between ISO 9001 and ISO 14001 standards; value added by the ISO 9001 standard; and lack of market demand for ISO 14001 compliance.

ISO 14001 System Overview

"ISO 14000 will be the most important international, non-regulatory, environmental standard of the 21st century. It will change the way we do business" (Mary McKiel, Director of U.S. EPA's Standards Networks). The ISO 14001 standard is an internationally accepted management standard used as a means of implementing and demonstrating a company's ability to continually improve operations, products and services with regard to the environment.

The ISO 14001 standard is comprised of six main clauses that are broken down into various sub-clauses. The six main clauses are as follows: General Requirements, Environmental Policy, Planning, Implementation and Operation, Checking and Corrective Action, and Management Review.

The commitment of executive management is an imperative to the success of an ISO 14001 system. The commitment means providing necessary resources and active support to make the environmental management system a reality. The environmental policy establishes direction and goals to reduce environmental degradation.

Planning is the critical aspect of the ISO 14001 system. The planning involves identifying positive and negative aspects and impacts of business as well as establishing objectives and targets. The objectives are goals to achieve for certain aspects, and targets are desired results. The identification of aspects should cover processes, products, services, operations, facilities, supplies and subcontracted operations. The objectives are prioritized for actions to achieve targets within a specified time. The objectives, targets and plans are routinely reviewed for progress and suitability.

Implementation requires the use of qualified company resources in order to raise awareness of environmental issues and implement actions to achieve objectives and targets. The processes are designed to reduce waste and prevent pollution. Communication of environmental intent of internal and external stakeholders is quite important to maintain accountability and demonstrate commitment to the environmental policy. Documentation required to implement ISO 14001 is continuation of the quality management system, where the environmental focus is added to existing procedures, and new procedures are developed to ensure compliance to the requirements.

Some of the additional processes that need to be documented include the following: environmental planning, communication, legal and other requirements, environmental audits, environmental training, and emergency preparedness and response. Operations controls are normally in place to monitor process performance; however, new operations control may need to be identified from an environmental viewpoint. Emergency preparedness and response addresses the handling of accidental incidents leading to safety, environmental hazards, ecosystem effects and accidental releases.

Measuring and monitoring ensure that the company's processes are performing in accordance with the stated policy, procedures and standard requirements. The data are collected at various operations to monitor process performance and are evaluated and acted upon to achieve desired targets. Environmental audits are conducted to determine conformance to the planned arrangements.

Management review in ISO 14001 is similar to the management review within the ISO 9000 system. The intent is to periodically review the performance of the ISO 14001 system and act upon the opportunities for improving environmental performance. The corrective and preventive action system is used to remedy nonconformances and address opportunities for improvement. The management review is used to assess the effectiveness of the environmental policy, objectives and targets, environmental audits, and corrective and preventive actions. The management review also provides a good time to review necessary changes to be made in the environmental management system.

Benefits of ISO 14001

Several electronics companies, including Sony, Xerox, Hitachi, Siemens, IBM, Oki, Digital Equipment, Motorola, Phillips, Apple, Lucent and Circuit Systems, have implemented ISO 14001 management systems. IBM, which earned a worldwide registration, has experienced improvements in its bottom line. Xerox has reported annual savings of about $200M.

The Lucent Microelectronics' system was designed to give a bigger picture of environmental performance as well as cost for all facilities. Oki's ISO 14001 project almost paid for itself by the time certification was achieved. Oki's benefits included reduced water consumption and a reduction in the production of hazardous treatment chemicals.

Most improvements stem from the operations' analysis for aspects and impacts. By reviewing operations, support functions, facilities and the supply chain against the environmental intent, a company can identify many opportunities for improvement.

Sumitomo Insurance Company announced that it would provide reduced rates for environmental impairment liability coverage by as much as 30% for ISO 14001 certified companies (The ISO Edge, Volume 3, Issue 1, 1999).

Comparatively speaking, ISO 9001 systems provide the following advantages:

- ➤ Establish an infrastructure to do business
- ➤ Establish quality focus and measurements
- ➤ Document process and process controls
- ➤ Focus on quality improvement
- ➤ Auditing for continuous improvement and compliance
- ➤ Reviews for effectiveness and business sense
- ➤ Reduction primarily in the product-related waste

ISO 14001 will add the following advantages:

- ➤ Supplement quality improvement
- ➤ Focus on waste reduction
- ➤ Increased awareness of environmental issues
- ➤ Reduced detrimental impact on environment

Utilizing the above, a company can improve operational efficiency and reduce waste for significant savings. Typical operational waste figures are about 30% of the revenues.

Implementing an ISO 14001 System

To implement a cost-effective ISO 14001 system, the following steps must be taken:

- ➤ Establish purpose and need for implementing an ISO 14001 management system.
- ➤ Document executive commitment in terms of resources and personal effort.
- ➤ Designate a champion to lead the ISO 14001 system. This person must be qualified and receive appropriate training.
- ➤ Review existing management practices. It is preferred to have an ISO 9001 management system first, as it creates

the business management infrastructure. However, one can implement ISO 14001 without having ISO 9001. In that case, the entire system will be implemented, including elements of ISO 9000.

- Conduct a gap analysis and identify areas that need to be addressed.
- Develop an implementation plan. The plan must address the following:
  - Training
  - Documentation
  - Implementation
  - Audits
- Train employees in the requirements of the standards and internal procedures.
- Document policy and procedures for addressing various requirements and business needs.
- Determine the environmental aspects and impacts throughout the facility, both inside and outside. This may take weeks or months. This is the most distinct and value-added step and will lead to significant savings.
- Train employees and management in following the documented environmental management system.
- Conduct internal environmental audits and remedy nonconformances.
- Schedule third-party audits and achieve certification.

Select a registrar with a great deal of experience auditing management systems. Have the registrar conduct a preliminary audit to obtain an objective view of the system's strengths and weaknesses before it counts toward registration. After remedying any preliminary audit findings and practicing the system for at least three months, a registration audit is scheduled, which should lead to certification of the ISO 14001 environmental management system. Internal audits of all clauses must be completed prior to the registration audit.

Since the external drivers for 14001 have not been strong, the acceptance in the PWB industry, for example, has been slow. A PWB company already complies with the applicable environmental regulations regarding waste discharge. However, the regulatory compliance does not encourage voluntary reduction in waste throughout operations. The benefits of compliance are lack of punishment by the applicable regulatory agency at a significant cost. The ISO 14001 system provides a mechanism to recover the cost of maintaining compliance and beyond through a reduction of material waste in operations. This reduction of material waste in operations thus impacts the environment via reduced discharge to the ecosystem, and most importantly, reduced fines by the regulatory agency.

In order for a company to implement the ISO 14001 system, the main challenge is to identify environmental aspects and their impact on the environment. Then, establishing a target to improve current performance will be perceived unnecessary due to lack of external demand for it. The environmental aspects are considered with respect to their release in the environment, resource conservation, regulations, impact on the community, and employee health and safety.

For example, in the Printed Wiring Board (PWB) industry, most of the solid or liquid discharges are regulated by governmental agencies, but a company must still identify them as environmental aspects and establish objectives and targets for impact reduction on the environment. The aspects may include the following: accidental spills, the presence of fiberglass dust in the drilling area, scrap boards, the use of paper and packaging material, discharge at de-burring, fumes exhaust and chemical discharge at wet processes, strip solution, photo film disposal, copper discharge at etching, rags and paper at screening, and waste water throughout the manufacturing. In addition to the environmental aspects in the manufacturing area, the environmental aspects are also identified throughout the non-manufacturing area.

Once a comprehensive list of environmental aspects is formulated, the aspects are prioritized based upon their impact on the environment, technology and legal implication. For key aspects, objectives and targets are established, and plans are developed, to reduce their environmental impact.

Questions to consider:

Why should my company seek ISO 14001 certification?

➢ Improved environmental performance
➢ Integration of environmental practices into the business
➢ Satisfy customer requirements
➢ Reduce waste and improve profitability

Which certification should my organization pursue first: ISO 9001 or ISO 14001?

I would recommend implementation of an ISO 9001 quality system first. The quality system allows a company to implement the necessary infrastructure to support business processes.

Can a company pursue both certifications at the same time?

The answer is 'yes,' because it could be easier and cheaper to integrate both during the development of management systems rather than implementing one after the other.

What are the costs and effort associated with ISO 9001 and ISO 14001 certifications?

The quality standard is harder to achieve, as it defines basic functions in the business, while the environmental standard adds requirements to the basic business functions. If the quality system is implemented first, the cost of implementing ISO 14001 could be 25% to 50% of the cost of implementing ISO 9001.

What benefits can we receive from ISO certifications?

The benefits include fewer spills, a reduced waste stream, less consumption and more pollution prevention. ISO 9001 and ISO 14001 together define excellence; they are two sides of a coin of excellence.

Conclusions

The ISO standards have credibility in the marketplace. Customers who are now asking for ISO 14000 compliance have demanded ISO 9000. The ISO 14000 movement is moving much faster than the ISO 9000 movement did, and it is being helped by the pre-existence of the ISO 9000 quality system. All companies should seriously consider ISO 14001 certification in order to compliment benefits of the quality system and improve profitability.

References

Michael Ross, Why Your Company Should Register to ISO 14001. Energy and Environmental Update, Volume 17, Number 2, 1997.

Praveen Gupta and Hans Upadhyay, Integrating Environmental and Quality Management Systems. ASQ 50th Congress Proceedings, May 1996.

Annette Dennis McCully, Rockwell Leverages ISO 14000 and ISO 9000 Management Systems. Quality Digest, April 1997.

Steve Freeman, How to prepare for an ISO 14001 Audit. Underwriters Laboratories, Inc. 1997.

Brian Lawrence, ISO 14001 – The New Environmental Management Paradigm. Environmental Technology, March/April 1997.

Editorial, The ISO Edge, Volume 3, Issue 1, pg. 2, 1st Quarter, 1999.

ISO 14000 Related Documents

ISO 14001: Environmental Management Systems – Specification with Guidance for Use

ISO 14011: Guidelines for Environmental Auditing

ISO 14020: Goals and Principles of Environmental Labeling

ISO 14031: Environmental Performance Evaluation – Guidelines

ISO 14040: Environmental Management – Life Cycle Assessment – Principles and Framework

ISO 14050: Terms and Definitions

Cost/Benefits of Implementing ISO 9001:2000

There is no doubt that ISO 9000 has gained considerable recognition over the past decade, as it has become the most widely recognized quality standard to date. When the term ISO 9000 comes to mind, some may think of it as a truly beneficial quality system, or essential for good business. Others may think of the terms "paper monster" or "unnecessary evil." Still others view it as beneficial but burdensome.

Sometimes companies implement ISO/QS-9000 without much choice in the matter, because their customers are requiring it. There are, however, a good number of companies that have the liberty to decide on their own if ISO/QS-9000 is worth implementing for them. The two main factors that are weighed out in most cases are the benefits received compared to the dollars put out.

Figure 4 lists the ten most commonly stated benefits, in ascending order, according to a survey conducted by Quality Technology Company in 1998. The most commonly stated benefit, as might be expected, is improvement of the quality system.

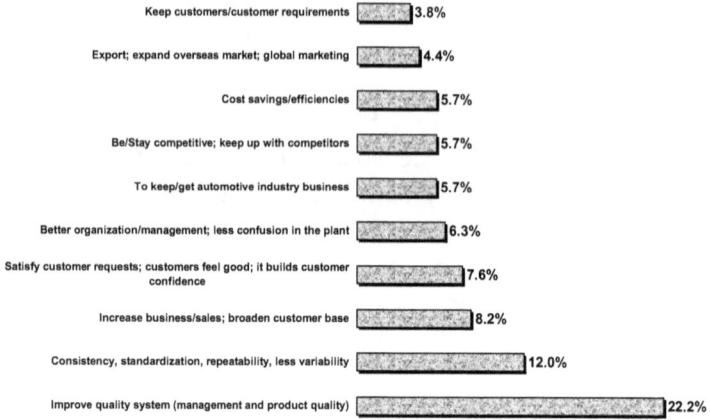

FIGURE 4: 10 MOST COMMONLY STATED BENEFITS

Keep customers/customer requirements — 3.8%

Export; expand overseas market; global marketing — 4.4%

Cost savings/efficiencies — 5.7%

Be/Stay competitive; keep up with competitors — 5.7%

To keep/get automotive industry business — 5.7%

Better organization/management; less confusion in the plant — 6.3%

Satisfy customer requests; customers feel good; it builds customer confidence — 7.6%

Increase business/sales; broaden customer base — 8.2%

Consistency, standardization, repeatability, less variability — 12.0%

Improve quality system (management and product quality) — 22.2%

The cost of implementing an ISO/QS-9000 system is shown in Figure 5. Of the certified companies, 44% spent over 150 thousand dollars, and only 14% were actually in the 30 to 60 thousand-dollar range.

FIGURE 5: COST OF IMPLEMENTING A QUALITY MANAGEMENT SYSTEM BASED ON THE COMPANY SIZE

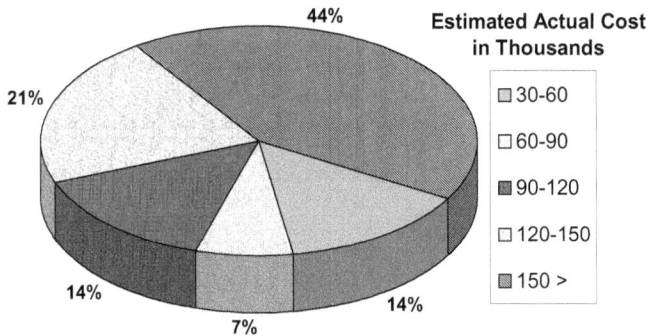

Implementation of ISO/QS-9000 can cost quite a bit of money, and maybe a lot more than expected. The good news is that the majority of participants in the survey believed that the ISO/QS-9000 system is a value-added system (see Figure 6).

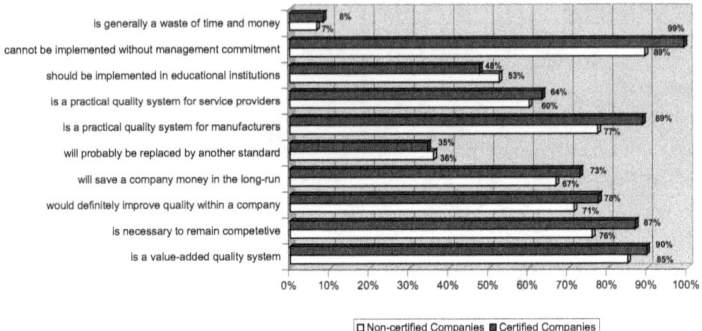

ISO/QS-9000:

With the release of the ISO 9001:2000 version, companies have three years to phase in the compliance to the new requirements. The cost-benefit analysis must consider the changes required for implementation of the quality management system effectively. The main changes that need to be considered are as follows:

➢ Restructure the quality management system
➢ Better system to control quality records
➢ Data analysis and corrective actions
➢ Business process maps
➢ Customer assessment
➢ Internal communication

The estimated cost of implementing the ISO 9001:2000 standard in existing organizations could vary as follows:

Company size	Number of employees	Estimated cost ($K)
Small	Less than 50	30 - 50
Medium	Between 51 – 250	75 - 100
Large	More than 250	100 - 150

The cost/investment to upgrade the quality management system includes the internal cost of internal resources for documentation, implementation and training, as well as the external costs of consulting and training. The ratio of internal and external costs could range from 50:50 to 70:30.

The fundamental benefit of implementing ISO 9001:2000 is improved effectiveness that has a direct bearing on profitability for the company. The improvement in effectiveness will be driven based on more regularly performed data analysis, identification of opportunities for improvement and resulting corrective actions leading to savings.

Top management must set goals to get benefits and value from implementing the quality management system. Otherwise, top management will just get a piece of paper certifying them for compliance. The ISO 9001:2000 version will not do anything for the company by itself; the top management must plan to utilize it through leadership, commitment, involvement and empowerment.

The ISO 9001:2000 version allows three years for currently certified companies to adapt to the new requirements. The main emphasis has shifted from documentation and compliance to effectiveness. The saying "Do what you say (document) and say (document) what you do" is not enough.

Instead, "Do well first, document it, do it repeatedly and then improve it" is required.

Conclusion

Identifying processes of the quality management system, monitoring them, and taking prompt corrective actions to maintain and improve them is a change more in the intent than in the language. The change is amplified through specifically requiring data analysis and making decisions based on facts. The internal audits and corrective actions must be implemented as intended, not as documented.

Completing corrective action paperwork will generate more corrective actions until the corrective action system is choked. Top management must review the effectiveness of internal audits and corrective actions. If these two elements are implemented effectively, other processes will improve automatically. Without implementing corrective action effectively, no matter how well the quality management system is implemented, it is bound to degrade, falter and disintegrate.

Involvement of top management cannot be over-emphasized. Management must believe that business performance is directly related to the performance of the quality management system. There is no function in the company that is not a part of the quality management system, nor should an attempt be made to exclude them from the quality management system.

Top management must define the business objectives that are critical or key indicators of the organization's performance. Even though management may have a good feel for the organization's performance, a system to track the performance and act upon it must be implemented. Top management's goal must be to manage the business through better leadership, planning, monitoring and communication. Its' employees will do the rest.

Empowering employees requires confidence in employees' capability. That confidence comes through effective recruitment, training, responsibility, accountability and trust. Without accountability, responsibility and trust, it is impossible to grow a business, reduce waste, and achieve better returns on investments. Good quality records are not only evidence of compliance; they also include secrets to growth and success.

The ISO 9001:2000 standard has been changed to emphasize collection and analysis of good information to achieve quality (business) objectives. This version also specifically focuses on ensuring the effectiveness of the quality system's implementation. With the release of ISO 9001:2000, companies should find it easier to achieve ISO 14001 certification, as the language of the new ISO 9001:2000 standard is much more compatible with ISO 14001.

NOTES